CODEX SIN

The Discovery of the World's Oldest Bible

Also Includes
The Mount Sinai Manuscript of the Bible
by the Trustees of the British Museum

Dr. Constantine Tischendorf

THE BOOK TREE
San Diego, California

Eighth Edition
originally published 1934
The Lutterworth Press
London, England

The Mount Sinai Manuscript of the Bible
Third Edition
Originally published 1934 for the
Trustees of the British Museum
London, England

ISBN 978-1-58509-367-0

Cover layout
Mike Sparrow

Cover Image
page from The Codex Sinaiticus
LUKE XXII, 36-52

Published by
The Book Tree
P.O. Box 16476
San Diego, CA 92176
www.thebooktree.com

We provide fascinating and educational products to help awaken the public to new ideas and
information that would not be available otherwise.
Call 1 (800) 700-8733 for our *FREE BOOK TREE CATALOG*.

INTRODUCTION

The author of this book, Constantine Tischendorf, was one of the world's leading biblical scholars of his time. He spent much of his life searching for ancient biblical manuscripts, with his primary goal being to provide the world with the earliest scriptures in existence. Starting in 1844 Tischedorf's greatest discovery was made. While visiting St. Catherine's monastery in the Sinai, he found what would later be confirmed as the oldest complete New Testament bible ever found. Most of the Old Testament was included as well. This book is his entire first-hand account of this amazing discovery, followed by his assessment of its historical importance. It took him three trips, altogether, to convince those in the monastery to trust him and allow this bible to be shared with the world. Most of it was brought to Russia, but it was later sold to the British Museum in 1933 after they bought it from the Russian government for 100,000 British pounds. *The Mount Sinai Manuscript of the Bible*, also included here in this Book Tree edition, was written shortly after the arrival of the manuscript in England. It outlines the known history of this bible and its importance to the world. Today, after years of study by scholars, this codex has revealed what the original scriptures may have looked like and what portions could have been later added.

It is estimated to have been completed sometime around 350 AD in beautiful, hand-written Greek text. Some scholars believe it resulted from Emperor Constantine's known decision to codify, once and for all, the books of Christianity after he had converted and adopted the religion into his regime. It was ordered to collect all books that were to be included in the Bible, and place them in canonical order. Much of what we find today in our later biblical versions reflects what was collected here. However, the highly important notes and textual variations in the Codex Sinaiticus, as well as some different sequencing and inclusions, make it invaluable in studying the formation of the canon and of the religion itself. This codex was the work of three different scribes and was quite likely the very first large-bound book ever produced

– as opposed to scrolls or very small bound books which were in their infancy. Its place or origin remains unclear, but one of its later editors puts it in Caesarea in the seventh century, due to a note made in the actual text. There was an important library in Caesarea in 350 AD up into the time this notation was made, but no solid proof exists to its location before this time. Its conjectured origin has been attributed to Alexandria, Egypt; Rome; and Southern Italy, among others. Despite these questions, the most important thing is the Codex itself.

The surviving manuscript today is scattered among four locations-those being St. Catherine's Monastery, Sinai (12 leaves and 14 fragments); the British Library (347 leaves); the University of Leipzig, Germany (43 leaves); and the National Library of Russia, St. Petersburg (fragments of 3 leaves). These four organizations began an international project in 2005 in an effort to accurately interpret it and make it accessible worldwide using digital technology, which was projected to be finished in 2009, and seems to have been made available in 2012 as an encoded XML file for researchers.

Interesting things have been found through the study of this text. Two examples: It has been reported that the Sinai version of the Gospel of Mark ends with Mary Magdalene arriving at the tomb of Jesus and finding it empty. This could call into question the resurrection story, as many other early bibles fail to contain it as well. Also, it has long been thought that that the Gospel of John originally ended at verse 21:24. Using ultra-violet light on the Codex, it was shown that verse 25 had once been there, but was removed because an early editor felt the same way as many modern scholars-that verse 25 was an interpolation and did not belong there. It is this type of thing that the joint project, mentioned above, was to be doing; however, combing though its huge size of about 28 million characters in order to find them, or in some cases finding and learning to use the proper tools to accomplish this, could be a challenge. For the average person and scholar alike, this book provides an interesting overview of the discovery and importance of this major document.

Paul Tice

CONTENTS

PREFACE TO EIGHTH EDITION

" I would rather have discovered this Sinaitic manuscript than the Koh-i-noor of the Queen of England," so said an eminent scholar when Oxford and Cambridge Universities conferred degrees on Dr. Tischendorf.

EVERY lover of the Bible has been thrilled by the new national acquisition in the British Museum. The story of the discoveries by the celebrated scholar in 1844 and 1859 is here related in his own words, together with the argument which he built thereupon as to the date of composition of the four Gospels. If Dr. Tischendorf were alive to-day he would doubtless express himself somewhat differently concerning such subjects as the Acts of Pilate and St. John's Gospel. The *Didache* (*Teaching of the Twelve*) was not discovered by Bryennios of Nicomedia till a quarter of a century later. But readers will be interested to compare the statements of seventy years ago with the theological outlook of the present time and to judge for themselves how much or how little the main positions are affected by the findings of modern scholarship.

If the transfer of the Codex Sinaiticus from Russia to London will help to stimulate the British people to a renewed personal, individual and family interest in the teaching of God's Word, it will be worth £100,000 many times over ; and this, quite apart from the satisfaction of having so valuable a manuscript housed at the centre of the Empire.

Contributions towards the cost of the Codex will be gladly received at this office, and will be forwarded to the proper authorities.

R. MERCER WILSON.

TRANSLATOR'S PREFACE

THE name of Dr. Constantine Tischendorf is too well known to need any introduction to the English reader. As a critic and decipherer of ancient manuscripts he was without a rival, and to his other services in this important department of sacred literature he added one which, alone, would reward the labour of a lifetime, in the discovery of the Sinaitic Manuscript, the full particulars of which are given to the English reader in the following pages.

The original pamphlet of Dr. Tischendorf, *Wann wurden unsere Evangelien verfasset*, attracted great attention on its first publication ; but as it was written in the technical style in which German professors are accustomed to address their students and the learned classes generally, it was felt that a revision of this pamphlet, in a more popular form and adapted to general readers, would meet a want of the age. Dr. Tischendorf accordingly complied with this request, and prepared a popular version, in which the same arguments for the genuineness and authenticity of our Gospels were reproduced, but in a style more attractive to general readers, and with explanations which clear up what would otherwise be unintelligible. Of this revised and popular version of his proof of the genuineness of our Gospels the following is an accurate translation.

It may interest the reader to know that the pamphlet in its popular form has passed through several large impressions in Germany : it has also been twice translated into French ; one version of which is by Professor Sardinoux, for the Religious Book Society of Toulouse. It has also been translated into Dutch and Russian ;

and an Italian version at Rome was undertaken by an Archbishop of the Church of Rome, and with the approbation of the Pope. We have only to add that this version into English was undertaken with the express approbation of the Author, and is sent forth in the hope that, with the Divine blessing, it may be instrumental in confirming the faith of many of our English readers in the " certainty of those things in which they have been instructed." If the foundations be overthrown, what shall the righteous do? On the four Gospels Christianity very much depends for its most momentous truths and facts. Hence it is that the Infidel and the Deist, with their unnatural ally the rationalizing Christian professor, have directed their attacks to the task of sapping these foundations. How unsuccessful as yet these repeated attempts of negative criticism have been, may be seen from the fact that the assault is repeated again and again. Infidelity, we are sure, would not waste her strength in thrice slaying the slain, or in raking away the ruins of a structure which has been demolished already. If the objections of Paulus and Eichhorn had been successful, the world would never have heard of Baur and the school of Tübingen. And again, if the Tübingen school had prevailed, there would not have been any room for the labours of such destructive critics as Volckmar of Zurich and others. The latest attack is, we are told, to be the last, until it fails, and another is prepared more threatening than the former. Thus every wave which beats against the rock of eternal truth seems to rise out of the trough caused by some receding wave, and raises its threatening crest as if it would wash away the rock. These waves of the sea are mighty, and rage terribly, but the Lord who sitteth on high is mightier. It is of the nature of truth, that the more it is tested the more sure it becomes under the trial. So it has been with the argument for the genuineness of the Gospels. The more that infidels have sought to shake the character of St. John's Gospel, the more collateral proofs have started up of the apostolic character of this Gospel. Thus, though they mean it not so, these attacks of opponents are among the means whereby fresh evidences of the certitude of the Gospels are called out. No one contributed more to this department of Christian literature than Dr. Tischendorf. This is an age when little books on great subjects are in larger request than ever. No defence of truth can therefore be more serviceable than the following short pamphlet, in which, in a few pages, and in a clear and attractive style, the genuineness of the Gospels is traced up inductively, step by step, almost, if not quite, to the days of the apostles.

The method of proof is one which is thoroughly satisfactory, and carries the convictions of the reader along with it at every step. Circumstantial evidence, when complete, and when every link in the chain has been thoroughly tested, is as strong as direct testimony. This is the kind of evidence which Dr. Tischendorf brings for the genuineness of our Gospels.

By what logicians call the method of rejection, it is shown successively that the Gospels which were admitted as canonical in the fourth century could not have been written so late as the third century after Christ. Then, in the same way, the testimony of the third century carries us up to the second. The writers, again, of the second century not only refer to the Gospels as already commonly received as parts of Sacred Scripture, but also refer their origin to a date not later than the end of the first century.

The induction is thus complete, that these writings which the earliest of the apostolic fathers refer to, and quote as apostolic writings, must have had their origin in apostolic times. Thus we see, that of all theories, the most irrational is that of the Rationalists, who have so often maintained that the Gospel of St. John was not written before the middle of the second century, and by a writer who palmed himself off as the Apostle John. We are at a loss to understand how the Church of the second century could have been so simple as not to detect the forgery—as it did in the case of so-called Apocryphal Gospels. The Rationalists give us no explanation of this, but would have us believe, on grounds of pure subjective criticism, that the Deity of our Lord was a development of the second and third centuries, after that the earlier Ebionite view of Jesus of Nazareth had been mixed up with the Alexandrian doctrine of the Logos : and that, as an amalgam of these two elements, the one Jewish and the other Greek, there resulted the Athanasian doctrine of the fourth century.

The historical proofs of Dr. Tischendorf blow to pieces this unsubstantial structure of inner or subjective criticism. No English reader of common sense will hesitate for an instant to decide to which side the scale inclines. With that reverence for facts which is our English birthright, we should set one single documentary proof like that, for instance, of the Codex Muratori, referred to in the following pages, against all the subjective criticism of the Tübingen school. Too long has Germany dreamed away her faith in the historical Christ, under the sleeping potions of these critics of the idealist school, who, with Baur at their head, only apply to theology the desolating and destructive theory of Hegel, that thought, when it projects itself outward, produces things ; and that all things exist because they seem to exist.

With such a school of metaphysics to start from, it is easy to see what the results would be when applied to historical criticism. "As with an enchanter's wand," facts which inconveniently did not square with the professor's theory were waved away into thin air, and history became a kind of phantasmagoria, a series of dissolving views. But the "magic-lantern school," as it has been happily called, has been already discredited in Germany, and is not likely to take firm hold in this country. To complete their dicomfiture, the labours of such textuary critics as Dr. Tischendorf are invaluable : critical proofs such as his are all the more acceptable as coming from Germany. The goodness and wisdom of God are seen in this, that as negative criticism had struck its roots deepest in German soil, so from Germany it receives its deadliest blows. In nature, we know the antidote to certain poisons is found growing close beside the bane. In Corsica, for instance, the mineral springs of Orezza are considered a specific for the malaria fever produced in the plains below ; so healthy German criticism has done more than anything else to clear the air of the miasma caused by unhealthy speculation.

The results of a single discovery such as that of Tischendorf will neutralize to every unprejudiced mind all the doubts which subjective criticism has been able to raise as to the genuineness of St. John's Gospel. Thus it is that God's Word is tried to the uttermost, and because so tried and found true, His servants love it. If the doubting of Thomas was overruled to the confirmation of the faith of all the apostles, we see the reason why the subjective criticism of the Tübingen school has been allowed to sap, if it could, the evidence of the Gospel of St. John, in order that additional testimony should be brought from a convent on Mount Sinai to confirm us still more fully in "the certainty of those things in which we have been instructed."

THE TRANSLATOR.

THE DISCOVERY OF THE SINAITIC MANUSCRIPT

*

As the Conference of the Evangelical Church of Germany, held at Altenburg, in the month of September, 1864, turned its attention to certain recent works on the Life of Jesus, I was requested by my friends to put together a few thoughts on this important subject, and read them before the Congress. This I consented to do, and pointed out that M. Renan has taken strange liberties with the Holy Land ; and that the history of the early Church, as well as that of the sacred text, contains abundant arguments in reply to those who deny the credibility of the Gospel witness. My address was so favourably received by the Congress, that the Editor of the *Allgemeine Kirchenzeitung*, on June 3, 1863, made use of the following language : "I venture to say that no address has ever stirred our hearts like that short one of M. Tischendorf. As a critic he is here on ground on which he has no rival. When history speaks, it is the duty of philosophy to be silent."

Familiar as I am through my long studies with those facts which are best calculated to throw light on that great question which now agitates Christendom, I have thought it right to publish the sketch of the subject, hasty as it was, which I had prepared at Altenburg. My work, printed in the month of March, 1864, has been so favourably received, that in three weeks an edition of 2,000 copies has been exhausted : a second edition was brought out in May, and translations in French and English were also prepared.

At the same time, the Committee of the Religious Tract Society at Zwickau expressed a desire to circulate this pamphlet, provided it was recast and adapted for popular use. Although I had many other occupations, I could not but comply with their request, and without delay applied myself to the task of revising the pamphlet. I was glad of the opportunity of addressing in this way a class of readers whom my former writings had not reached ; for, as the real results of my researches are destined to benefit the Church at large, it is right that the whole community should participate in those benefits.

This popular tract, in the shape in which I now publish it, lacks, I admit, the simple and familiar style of the usual publications of the Zwickau Society ; but, in spite of this fault, which the very nature of the subject renders inevitable, I venture to hope that it will be generally understood. Its chief aim is to show that our inspired Gospels most certainly take their rise from apostolic times, and so to enable the reader to take a short but clear view of one of the most instructive and important epochs of the Christian Church.

In sitting down to write a popular version of my pamphlet, the Zwickau Society also expressed a wish that I should preface it with a short account of my researches, and especially of the discovery of the Sinaitic Codex, which naturally takes an important place in my list of documentary proofs. The account of these discoveries is already before the public, but as it is possibly new to many of those who read the Zwickau publications, I yielded to the wish of the Committee, having no other desire in this attempt than to build up my readers in their most holy faith.

As several literary and historical essays, written by me when a very young man, and in particular two theological prize essays, were favourably received by the public, I resolved, in 1839, to devote myself to the textual study of the New Testament, and attempted, by making use of all the acquisitions of the last three centuries, to reconstruct, if possible, the exact text, as it came from the pen of the sacred writers. My first critical edition of the New Testament appeared in the autumn of 1840. But after giving this edition a final revision, I came to the conviction that to make use even of our existing materials would call for a more attentive study than they had hitherto received, and I resolved to give my leisure and abilities to a fresh examination of the original documents. For the accomplishment of this protracted and difficult enterprise, it was needful not only to undertake distant journeys, to devote much time, and to bring to the task both ability and zeal, but also to provide a large sum of money, and this—the sinews of war—was altogether wanting. The Theological Faculty of Leipzig gave me a letter of recommendation to the Saxon Government ; but at first without any result. Doctor Von Falkenstein, however, on being made Minister of Public Worship, obtained a grant for me of 100 thalers (about £15) to defray my travelling expenses, and a promise of another hundred for the following year. What was such a sum as this with which to undertake a long journey? Full of faith, however, in the proverb that " God helps those who help themselves," and that what is right must prosper, I resolved, in 1840, to set out for Paris (on the very day of the Feast of the Reformation), though I had not sufficient means to pay even for my travelling suit ; and when I reached Paris I had only fifty thalers left. The other fifty had been spent on my journey.

However, I soon found men in Paris who were interested in my undertaking. I managed for some time to support myself by my pen, keeping, however, the object which had brought me to Paris steadily in view. After having explored for two years the rich libraries of this great city, not to speak of several journeys made into Holland and England, I set out

in 1843 for Switzerland, and spent some time at
Basle. Then passing through the south of France I
made my way into Italy, where I searched the libraries
of Florence, Venice, Modena, Milan, Verona, and
Turin. In April, 1844, I pushed on to the East.
Egypt and the Coptic convents of the Libyan desert,
Mount Sinai in Arabia, Jerusalem, Bethlehem, and
the Convent of St. Saba on the shores of the Dead
Sea, Nazareth and its neighbourhood, Smyrna and
the island of Patmos, Beyrout, Constantinople, Athens ;
these were the principal points of my route, and of my
researches in the East. Lastly, having looked in on
my way home on the libraries of Vienna and Munich,
I returned to Leipzig in January, 1845.

This journey cost me 5,000 thalers (£750). You
are ready to ask me, how the poor traveller, who
set out from Leipzig with only a few uncashed bills,
could procure such sums as these. I have already
partly given you a clue to explain this, and will more
fully account for it as we go on with the narrative.
Such help as I was able to offer to fellow-travellers,
a great deal of kindness in return, and, above all,
that enthusiasm which does not start back from priva-
tions and sacrifices, will explain how I got on. But
you are naturally more anxious to hear what those
labours were to which I devoted five years of my life.

With this view I return to that edition of the New
Testament of which I have spoken above. Soon after
the Apostles had composed their writings, they began
to be copied ; and the incessant multiplication of
copy upon copy went on down to the sixteenth century,
when printing happily came to replace the labour of
the copyist. One can easily see how many errors
must have inevitably crept into writings which were
so often reproduced ; but it is more difficult still to
understand, how writers could allow themselves to

18

bring in here and there changes, not verbal only, but such as materially affect the meaning, and, what is worse still, did not shrink from cutting out a passage or inserting one.

The first editions of the Greek text, which appeared in the sixteenth century, were based upon manuscripts which happened to be the first to come to hand. For a long time men were satisfied to reproduce and reprint these early editions. In this way there arose a disposition to claim for this text, so often reprinted, a peculiar value, without ever caring to ask whether it was an exact reproduction or not of the actual text as it was written in the first century. But in the course of time manuscripts were discovered in the public libraries of Europe which were a thousand years old, and on comparing them with the printed text, critics could not help seeing how widely the received text departed in many places from the text of the manuscripts. We should also here add that from the very earliest age of the Christian era the Greek text had been translated into different languages—into Latin, Syriac, Egyptian, etc. Ancient manuscripts of these versions were also brought to light, and it was impossible not to see what variation of readings there had been in the sacred text. The quotations made by the Fathers, from as early as the second century, also confirmed in another way the fact of these variations. It has thus been placed beyond doubt that the original text of the Apostles' writings, copied, recopied, and multiplied during fifteen centuries, whether in Greek or Latin, or in other languages, had in many passages undergone such serious modifications of meaning as to leave us in painful uncertainty as to what the Apostles had actually written.

Learned men have again and again attempted to clear the sacred text from these extraneous elements.

But we have at last hit upon a better plan even than this, which is to set aside this *textus receptus* altogether, and to construct a fresh text, derived immediately from the most ancient and authoritative sources. This is undoubtedly the right course to take, for in this way only can we secure a text approximating as closely as possible to that which came from the Apostles.

Now to obtain this we must first make sure of our ground by thoroughly studying the documents which we possess. Well, in completing my first critical edition of the New Testament, in 1840, I became convinced that the task, so far from completed, was little more than begun, although so many and such celebrated names are found on the list of critical editors ; to mention only a few out of many : Erasmus, Robert Stephens, Beza, Mill, Wetstein, Bengel, Griesbach, Matthæi, and Scholz. This conviction led me to begin my travels. I formed the design of revising and examining, with the utmost possible care, the most ancient manuscripts of the New Testament which were to be found in the libraries of Europe ; and nothing seemed to me more suitable, with this end in view, than to publish with the greatest exactness the most important of these documents. I should thus secure the documents as the common property of Christendom, and ensure their safe keeping by men of learning, should the originals themselves ever happen to perish.

I extended, for this reason, my investigations to the most ancient Latin manuscripts, on account of their great importance, without passing by the Greek text of the Old Testament, which was referred to by the Apostles in preference to the original Hebrew, and which, notwithstanding its high authority, had during the lapse of two thousand years become more corrupt than that of the New Testament. I extended my researches also to the Apocryphal books of the New Testament, as the present treatise will readily show. These works bear upon the canonical books in more respects than one, and throw a considerable light on Christian antiquity. The greater number of them were buried in our great libraries, and it is doubtful if any one of them had received the attention which it deserved. In the next place, I proposed to collect together all the Greek manuscripts which we possess, which are of a thousand years' antiquity, including in the list even those which do not bear on the Bible, so as to exhibit in a way never before done, when and how the different manuscripts had been written. In this way we should be better able to understand why one manuscript is to be referred to the fourth century, another to the fifth, and a third to the eighth, although they had no dates attached to determine when they were written.

Such then have been the various objects which I hoped to accomplish by my travels. To some, all this may seem mere learned labour : but permit me to add that the science touches on life in two important respects ; to mention only two,—to clear up in this way the history of the sacred text, and to recover if possible the genuine apostolic text which is the foundation of our faith,—these cannot be matters of small importance. The whole of Christendom is, in fact, deeply interested in these results. Of this there can be no doubt ; and the extraordinary proofs of interest that the Christian world has given me are alone a sufficient attestation.

The literary treasures which I have sought to explore have been drawn in most cases from the convents of the East, where, for ages, the pens of industrious monks have copied the sacred writings, and collected manuscripts of all kinds. It therefore occurred to me whether it was not probable that in some recess of Greek or Coptic, Syrian or Armenian monasteries, there might be some precious manuscripts slumbering for ages in dust and darkness ? And would not every sheet of parchment so found, covered with writings of the fifth, sixth, and seventh centuries, be a kind of literary treasure, and a valuable addition to our Christian literature ?

These considerations have, ever since the year 1842, fired me with a strong desire to visit the East. I had just completed at the time a work which had been very favourably received in Europe, and for which I had received marks of approval from several learned bodies, and even from crowned heads.

The work I advert to was this. There lay in one of the libraries of Paris one of the most important manuscripts then known of the Greek text. This parchment manuscript, the writing of which, of the date of the fifth century, had been retouched and renewed in the seventh, and again in the ninth century, had, in the twelfth century, been submitted to a twofold process. It had been washed and pumiced, to write on it the treatises of an old father of the Church of the name of Ephrem. Five centuries later, a Swiss theologian of the name of Wetstein had attempted to decipher a few traces of the original manuscript ; and, later still, another theologian, Griesbach of Jena, came to try his skill on it, although the librarian assured him that it was impossible for mortal eye to decipher a writing which had disappeared for six centuries. In spite of these unsuccessful attempts, the French Government had recourse to powerful chemical reagents, to bring out the effaced characters. But a Leipzig theologian, who was then at Paris, was so unsuccessful in this new attempt, that he asserted that it was impossible to produce an edition of this text, as the manuscript was quite illegible. It was after all these attempts that I began, in 1841-2, to try my skill at the manuscript, and had the good fortune to decipher it completely, and even to distinguish between the dates of the different writers who had been engaged on the manuscript.

This success, which procured for me several marks of recognition and support, encouraged me to proceed. I conceived it to be my duty to complete an undertaking which had hitherto been treated as chimerical. The Saxon Government came forward to support me. The king, Frederick Augustus II, and his distinguished brother, John, sent me marks of their approval ; and several eminent patrons of learning at Frankfort, Geneva, Rome, and Breslau generously offered to interest themselves in my attempt.

I here pass over in silence the interesting details of my travels—my audience with the Pope, Gregory XVI, in May, 1843—my intercourse with Cardinal Mezzofanti, that surprising and celebrated linguist—and I come to the result of my journey to the East. It was in April, 1844, that I embarked at Leghorn for Egypt. The desire which I felt to discover some precious remains of any manuscripts, more especially Biblical, of a date which would carry us back to the early times of Christianity, was realized beyond my expectations. It was at the foot of Mount Sinai, in the Convent of St. Catherine, that I discovered the pearl of all my researches. In visiting the library of the monastery, in the month of May, 1844, I perceived in the middle of the great hall a large and wide basket full of old parchments ; and the librarian, who was a man of information, told me that two heaps of papers like these, mouldered by time, had been already committed to the flames. What was my surprise to find amid this heap of papers a considerable number of sheets of a copy of the Old Testament in Greek, which seemed to me to be one of the most ancient that I had ever seen. The authorities of the convent allowed me to possess myself of a third of these parchments, or about forty-three sheets, all the more readily as they were destined for the fire. But I could not get them to yield up possession of the remainder. The too lively satisfaction which I had displayed had aroused their suspicions as to the value of this manuscript. I transcribed a page of the text of Isaiah and Jeremiah, and enjoined on the monks to take religious care of all such remains which might fall in their way.

On my return to Saxony there were men of learning who at once appreciated the value of the treasure which I brought back with me. I did not divulge the name of the place where I had found it, in the hopes of returning and recovering the rest of the manuscript. I handed over to the Saxon Government my rich collection of Oriental manuscripts in return for the payment of all my travelling expenses. I deposited in the library of the University of Leipzig, in shape of a collection, which bears my name, fifty manuscripts, some of which are very rare and interesting. I did the same with the Sinaitic fragments, to which I gave the name of Codex Frederick Augustus, in acknowledgment of the patronage given to me by the King of Saxony ; and I published them in Saxony in a sumptuous edition, in which each letter and stroke was exactly reproduced by the aid of lithography.

But these home labours upon the manuscripts which I had already safely garnered did not allow me to forget the distant treasure which I had discovered. I made use of an influential friend, who then resided at the Court of the Viceroy of Egypt, to carry on negotiations for procuring the rest of the manuscripts ;

but his attempts were, unfortunately, not successful. "The monks of the convent," he wrote to me to say, "have, since your departure, learned the value of these sheets of parchment, and will not part with them at any price."

I resolved, therefore, to return to the East to copy this priceless manuscript. Having set out from Leipzig in January, 1853, I embarked at Trieste for Egypt, and in the month of February I stood for the second time in the Convent of Sinai. This second journey was more successful even than the first, from the discoveries that I made of rare Biblical manuscripts ; but I was not able to discover any further traces of the treasure of 1844. I forget : I found in a roll of papers a little fragment which, written over on both sides, contained eleven short lines of Genesis, which convince me that the manuscript originally contained the entire Old Testament, but that the greater part had been long since destroyed.

On my return, I reproduced in the first volume of a collection of ancient Christian documents the page of the Sinaitic manuscript which I had transcribed in 1844, without divulging the secret of where I had found it. I confined myself to the statement that I claimed the distinction of having discovered other documents—no matter whether published in Berlin or Oxford—as I assumed that some learned travellers, who had visited the convent after me, had managed to carry them off.

The question now arose how to turn to use these discoveries. Not to mention a second journey which I made to Paris in 1849, I went through Germany, Switzerland, and England, devoting several years of unceasing labour to a seventh edition of my New Testament. But I felt myself more and more urged to recommence my researches in the East. Several motives, and more especially the deep reverence of all Eastern monasteries for the Emperor of Russia, led me, in the autumn of 1856, to submit to the Russian Government a plan of a journey for making systematic researches in the East. This proposal only aroused a jealous and fanatical opposition in St. Petersburg. People were astonished that a foreigner and a Protestant should presume to ask the support of the Emperor of the Greek and Orthodox Church for a mission to the East. But the good cause triumphed. The interest which my proposal excited, even within the imperial circle, inclined the Emperor in my favour. It obtained his approval in the month of September, 1858, and the funds which I asked for were placed at my disposal. Three months subsequently my seventh edition of the New Testament, which had cost me three years of incessant labour, appeared ; and in the commencement of January, 1859, I again set sail for the East.

I cannot here refrain from mentioning the peculiar satisfaction I had experienced a little before this. A learned Englishman, one of my friends, had been sent into the East by his Government to discover and purchase old Greek manuscripts, and spared no cost in obtaining them. I had cause to fear, especially for my pearl of the Convent of St. Catherine ; but I heard that he had not succeeded in acquiring anything, and had not even gone as far as Sinai—" for," as he said in his official report, " after the visit of such an antiquarian and critic as Dr. Tischendorf, I could not expect any success." I saw by this how well advised I had been to reveal to no one my secret of 1844.

By the end of the month of January I had reached the Convent of Mount Sinai. The mission with which I was entrusted entitled me to expect every consideration and attention. The prior, on saluting me, expressed a wish that I might succeed in discovering fresh supports for the truth. His kind expression of goodwill was verified even beyond his expectations.

After having devoted a few days in turning over the manuscripts of the convent, not without alighting here and there on some precious parchment or other, I told my Bedouins, on the 4th February, to hold themselves in readiness to set out with their dromedaries for Cairo on the 7th, when an entirely fortuitous circumstance carried me at once to the goal of all my desires. On the afternoon of this day I was taking a walk with the steward of the convent in the neighbourhood, and as we returned, towards sunset, he begged me to take some refreshment with him in his cell. Scarcely had he entered the room, when, resuming our former subject of conversation, he said: " And I, too, have read a Septuagint "— *i.e.* a copy of the Greek translation made by the Seventy. And so saying, he took down from the corner of the room a bulky kind of volume, wrapped up in a red cloth, and laid it before me. I unrolled the cover, and discovered, to my great surprise, not only those very fragments which, fifteen years before, I had taken out of the basket, but also other parts of the Old Testament, the New Testament complete, and, in addition, the Epistle of Barnabas and a part of the Pastor of Hermas. Full of joy, which this time I had the self-command to conceal from the steward and the rest of the community, I asked, as if in a careless way, for permission to take the manuscript into my sleeping chamber to look over it more at leisure. There by myself I could give way to the transport of joy which I felt. I knew that I held in my hand the most precious Biblical treasure in existence—a document whose age and importance

27

exceeded that of all the manuscripts which I had ever examined during twenty years' study of the subject. I cannot now, I confess, recall all the emotions which I felt in that exciting moment with such a diamond in my possession. Though my lamp was dim, and the night cold, I sat down at once to transcribe the Epistle of Barnabas. For two centuries search has been made in vain for the original Greek of the first part of this Epistle, which has only been known through a very faulty Latin translation. And yet this letter, from the end of the second down to the beginning of the fourth century, had an extensive authority, since many Christians assigned to it and to the Pastor of Hermas a place side by side with the inspired writings of the New Testament. This was the very reason why these two writings were both thus bound up with the Sinaitic Bible, the transcription of which is to be referred to the first half of the fourth century, and about the time of the first Christian emperor.

Early on the 5th of February I called upon the steward. I asked permission to take the manuscript with me to Cairo, to have it there transcribed completely from beginning to end ; but the prior had set out only two days before also for Cairo, on his way for Constantinople, to attend at the election of a new archbishop, and one of the monks would not give his consent to my request. What was then to be done? My plans were quickly decided. On the 7th, at sunrise, I took a hasty farewell of the monks, in hopes of reaching Cairo in time to get the prior's consent. Every mark of attention was shown me on setting out. The Russian flag was hoisted from the convent walls, while the hillsides rang with the echoes of a parting salute, and the most distinguished members of the order escorted me on my way as far as the plain.

The following Sunday I reached Cairo, where I was received with the same marks of goodwill. The prior, who had not yet set out, at once gave his consent to my request, and also gave instructions to a Bedouin to go and fetch the manuscript with all speed. Mounted on his camel, in nine days he went from Cairo to Sinai and back, and on the 24th February the priceless treasure was again in my hands. The time was now come at once boldly and without delay to set to work to a task of transcribing no less than a hundred and ten thousand lines—of which a great number were difficult to read, either on account of later corrections, or through the ink having faded —and that in a climate where the thermometer during March, April, and May is never below 77° of Fahrenheit in the shade. No one can say what this cost me in fatigue and exhaustion.

The relation in which I stood to the monastery gave me the opportunity of suggesting to the monks the thought of presenting the original to the Emperor of Russia as the natural protector of the Greek Orthodox faith. The proposal was favourably entertained, but an unexpected obstacle arose to prevent its being acted upon. The new archbishop, unanimously elected during Easter week, and whose right it was to give a final decision in such matters, was not yet consecrated, or his nomination even accepted by the Sublime Porte. And while they were waiting for this double solemnity, the Patriarch of Jerusalem protested so vigorously against the election, that a three months' delay must intervene before the election could be ratified and the new archbishop installed. Seeing this, I resolved to set out for Jaffa and Jerusalem.

Just at this time the Grand-Duke Constantine of Russia, who had taken the deepest interest in my labours, arrived at Jaffa. I accompanied him to

Jerusalem. I visited the ancient libraries of the holy city, that of the monastery of Saint Saba on the shores of the Dead Sea, and then those of Beyrout, Ladikia, Smyrna, and Patmos. These fresh researches were attended with the most happy results. At the time desired I returned to Cairo ; but here, instead of success, only met with a fresh disappointment. The Patriarch of Jerusalem still kept up his opposition, and as he carried it to the most extreme lengths, the five representatives of the convent had to remain at Constantinople, where they sought in vain for an interview with the Sultan to press their rights. Under these circumstances the monks of Mount Sinai, although willing to do so, were unable to carry out my suggestion.

In this embarrassing state of affairs the archbishop and his friends entreated me to use my influence on behalf of the convent. I therefore set out at once for Constantinople, with a view of there supporting the case of the five representatives. The Prince Lobanow, Russian ambassador to Turkey, received me with the greatest goodwill, and as he offered me hospitality in his country house on the shores of the Bosphorus, I was able the better to attend to the negotiations which had brought me there. But our irreconcilable enemy, the influential and obstinate Patriarch of Jerusalem, still had the upper hand. The archbishop was then advised to appeal himself in person to the patriarchs, archbishops, and bishops ; and this plan succeeded—for before the end of the year the right of the convent was recognized, and we gained our cause. I myself brought back the news of our success to Cairo, and with it I also brought my own special request, backed with the support of Prince Lobanow.

On the 24th of September I returned to Cairo. The monks and archbishop then warmly expressed

30

their thanks for my zealous efforts in their cause, and the following day I received from them, under the form of a loan, the Sinaitic Bible, to carry it to St. Petersburg, and there to have it copied as accurately as possible.

I set out for Russia early in October, and on the 19th of November I presented to their Imperial Majesties, in the Winter Palace at Tsarkoe-Selo, my rich collection of old Greek, Syriac, Coptic, Arabic, and other manuscripts, in the middle of which the Sinaitic Bible shone like a crown. I then took the opportunity of submitting to the Emperor Alexander II a proposal of making an edition of this Bible worthy of the work and of the Emperor himself, and which should be regarded as one of the greatest undertakings in critical and Biblical study.

I did not feel free to accept the brilliant offers that were made to me to settle finally, or even for a few years, in the Russian capital. It was at Leipzig, therefore, at the end of three years, and after three journeys to St. Petersburg, that I was able to carry to completion the laborious task of producing a *facsimile* copy of this codex in four folio volumes.

In the month of October, 1862, I repaired to St. Petersburg to present this edition to their majesties. The Emperor, who had liberally provided for the cost, and who approved the proposal of this superb manuscript appearing on the celebration of the Millenary Jubilee of the Russian empire, has distributed impressions of it throughout the Christian world, which, without distinction of creed, have expressed their recognition of its value. Even the Pope, in an autograph letter, has sent to the editor his congratulations and admiration. The two most celebrated universities of England, Cambridge and Oxford, desired to show me honour by conferring on me their highest

academic degree. " I would rather," said an old
man—himself of the highest distinction for learning
—" I would rather have discovered this Sinaitic
manuscript than the Koh-i-noor of the Queen of
England."

But that which I think more highly of than all
these flattering distinctions is the fact that Providence
has given to our age, in which attacks on Christianity
are so common, the Sinaitic Bible, to be to us a full
and clear light as to what is the real text of God's
Word written, and to assist us in defending the truth
by establishing its authentic form.

WHEN WERE OUR GOSPELS WRITTEN?

CHAPTER I

ECCLESIASTICAL TESTIMONY

AND now what shall we say respecting the life of Jesus ? What do we certainly know on this subject ?

This question has been much discussed in our days. It is well known that several learned men have, quite recently, written works on the life of Jesus, purporting to prove that He whom Christendom claims as her Lord did not really live the life that the Gospels record of Him. These works, which have been very freely circulated, have found a large number of readers. It may be that there are some points not yet fully understood, but this at least is undeniable, that the tendency of the works referred to is to rob the Saviour of His Divine character.

But, perhaps, it will be said, " The Deity of Christ is not an essential element of Christianity. Does there not remain to us its sublime system of morals, even though Christ were not the Son of God ? " To reason in this way seems to us to imply either that we have no idea at all of what Christianity is, or, which comes to the same thing, that we have an essentially wrong idea. Christianity does not, strictly speaking, rest on the moral teaching of Jesus, however sublime that is, but it rests on His person only. It is on the person of Christ that the Church is founded ; this is its cornerstone ; it is on this the doctrines which Jesus and His apostles taught rest as the foundation truth of all. And if we are in error in believing in the person of Christ

33

as taught us in the Gospels, then the Church herself is in error, and must be given up as a deception.

The link then which unites the Church to the person of Christ is so close, that to determine the nature of that Person is to her the vital question of all. The Christian world is perfectly sure that it is so, nd I need appeal to no other fact than her anxiety to know all that can be known of the life of Jesus, since the nature of His person can only be known through His life.

All the world knows that our Gospels are succinct narratives of the life of Christ. We must also frankly admit that we have no other source of information with respect to the life of Jesus than the sacred writings. In fact, whatever the early ages of the Church report to us concerning the person of Christ from any independent source is either derived from the Gospels, or is made up of a few insignificant details of no value in themselves, or is sometimes drawn from hostile sources. These are the only sources from which opponents of the life of Christ, of His miraculous ministry, and His Divine character draw their attacks on the credibility of the four Gospels.

But it will then be said, how has it been possible to impugn the credibility of the Gospels—of these books which St. Matthew and St. John, the immediate disciples and apostles of the Lord, and St. Mark and St. Luke, the friends and companions of the apostles, have written?

It is in this way : by denying that the Gospels were written by the authors whose names they bear. And if you ask me, in the next place, why it is that so much stress is laid on this point, I will answer that the testimony of direct eye-witnesses, like John and Matthew, or of men intimately connected with these eye-witnesses, like Mark and Luke, is entitled, for this very reason, to be believed, and their writings to be received as trustworthy. The credibility of a writer clearly depends on the interval of time which lies between him and the events which he describes. The farther the narrator is removed from the facts which he lays before us, the more his claims to credibility are reduced in value. When a considerable space of time intervenes, the writer can only report to us what he has heard from intermediate witnesses, or read of in writers who are perhaps undeserving of credit. Now the opponents of our Gospels endeavour to assign them to writers of this class, who were not in a position to give a really credible testimony; to writers who only composed their narratives long after the time when Christ lived, by putting together all the loose reports which circulated about His person and work. It is in this way that they undermine the credit of the Gospels, by detaching them completely from the Evangelists whose names they bear.

This is certainly one most successful way of overturning the dignity and authority of the Gospels.

There is another plan even more likely to effect the same end, and which they have not failed to have recourse to. There are men who call themselves enlightened who think that common sense is quite superior to Divine Revelation, and who pretend to explain the miracles of Scripture, either by the imperfect ideas of these times, or by a certain prejudiced theory of the Old Testament, or by a sort of accommodation, according to which Jesus adapted His words and deeds to meet the hopes of the Jews, and so passed Himself off among them as something greater than He really was.

This exaltation of common sense is not without its attractions for men of the world. It is easily understood, and so, little by little, it has become our modern form of belief. Men have withdrawn themselves from God and Christianity, and it must be confessed that many of these empty and sonorous phrases about liberty and the dignity of man have contributed not a little to this result. " Do not believe," they will tell you, " that man is born in sin and needs to be redeemed. He has a nature which is free, and which has only to be elevated to all that is beautiful and good, in order that he may properly enjoy life." Once admit this, and it is easy to see that this kind of unbelief will soon make away with the Gospels, as well as the rest of the Scriptures. It will despise them as the expressions of an antiquated and bygone state of feeling, and will shake them off as cumbrous chains as soon as it can.

The volume which appeared in Paris in 1863, and which has since made such a stir in the world, *La Vie de Jésus*, by M. Renan, is one of the fruits of this unbelief. This work has nothing in common with those that loyally and honestly inquire into the facts of the case. It is written on most arbitrary principles of its own, and is nothing else than a caricature of history from beginning to end. Can we suppose, for instance, that M. Renan seriously believes his own theory, that St. John wrote his Gospel because his vanity was offended, either through jealousy of St. Peter or hatred of Judas ? Or, when he accounts for the interest of the wife of Pilate in Jesus in these terms, " That she had possibly seen the fair young Galilean from some window of the palace which opened on the Temple court. Or perhaps she saw Him in a dream, and the blood of the innocent young man who was about to be condemned gave her a nightmare." Again, when he attempts to explain the resurrection of Lazarus by a deception of this same Lazarus, which was afterwards found out by Jesus, and by an act of

36

extravagance of his sisters, which is excusable on account of their fanaticism. "Lazarus," M. Renan says, "yet pale with sickness, had himself wrapped up in grave clothes, and laid in the family sepulchre."

These examples, which we could easily add to if we did not wish to avoid giving our readers unnecessary pain, seem to us sufficient to give an idea of M. Renan's book ; and since, in spite of all its frivolity, its historical inconsistency, and its tasteless disfigurement of facts, this production has made, even in Germany, such an impression, is it not plain that, alas ! even among us, infidelity is widely diffused ?—partly produced by, and partly the cause, in return, of our ignorance of the history of the Bible.

For this book of Renan's, German criticism is in a certain sense responsible. The manner of handling the Bible which we have described already, and which consists in setting common sense above revelation, took its rise on the soil of Germany. M. Renan sets out with this principle, and there are not wanting learned men in Germany who endeavour to give it completeness, by supplying it with the scientific base which it wants. This leads us quite naturally to speak of the direct attacks against the authenticity and apostolic authority of the Gospels, though, as far as this French work is concerned, it is written in too thin and superficial a style to be of much account one way or the other, and would certainly not have much effect in shaking any thinking person in his belief in the Gospel, or cause him, without further inquiry, to give up the traditional view that the Gospels really came from the writers to whom the Church refers them.

To know what we are to believe in this matter we must carefully examine the proofs which our adversaries bring forward. The chief points in their case are the assertions which they make, and pretend to

37

support by the history of the second century—that the Gospels did not see the light till after the end of the apostolic age. To support this point, they appeal to the testimony of the most ancient Church literature. They maintain that the Christian writings composed immediately after the apostles do not show any trace of acquaintance with, nor use of, the Gospels, which we possess, and especially with that of St. John, and they conclude that the Gospels could not, consequently, have been in existence.

If this assertion of theirs is well founded, if there exists such a Christian literature as they speak of,— that is, a series of works written between the end of the first century and the middle of the second,—and if we do not find in these writings any reference to our Gospels, then I should admit that the faith of the Church, which teaches that the Gospels were written during the second half of the first century, would be seriously compromised. Against such an assertion as this we could only raise one objection : we should ask if the nature and extent of the literature absolutely and inevitably required that it should refer to and quote the Gospels, and whether we should be entitled, from its silence on the subject of the Gospels, to claim such an inference as this ?—for it is conceivable that many excellent things might have been written on the subject without any direct reference to the Gospels. But what could we say if we had to prove the direct contrary ? I mean, if we were to find in works written a little after the apostolic age direct quotations from the Gospels ; or if we see them treated with the greatest respect, or perhaps even already treated as canonical and sacred writings ? In this case it would be beyond doubt that our Gospels would have been really composed in the apostolic age—a conclusion which our opponents resist and deny with all their might.

The writer of this pamphlet, in common with many other impartial critics, is firmly convinced that a conscientious examination of the question proves precisely the very opposite to that which the adversaries of the Gospel affirm : and this is especially true of the Gospel of St. John, the most important of the four. To throw light on this important question, we must enter without delay on this inquiry, and ascertain as clearly as possible whether the most primitive Christian literature bears any testimony for or against our Evangelists.

To do this, let us transport ourselves back to the latter half of the second century, and inquire how the Christian Church of that day thought of the four Evangelic narratives.

The first thing which strikes us is, that in all parts of the Church the four Evangelists were treated as a part of Holy Scripture. The Church Fathers of that age, belonging to many different countries, have written works in which they are very frequently quoted, and are always treated as sacred and apostolic writings.

At Lyons, where the first Christian Church in Gaul was founded, the Bishop Irenæus wrote, before the end of the second century, a great work on those early Gnostic heresies which arbitrarily attempted to overturn the doctrine of the Church : and in combating these errors he made a general use of the Gospels. The number of the passages which he refers to is about *four hundred*, and the direct quotations from St. John alone exceed eighty.

We may say as much for the energetic and learned Tertullian, who lived at Carthage about the end of the second century. His numerous writings contain several hundred pages taken from the Gospels—two hundred of these, at least, from St. John.

It is the same with Clement, the celebrated teacher of the Catechetical School of Alexandria, in Egypt, who also lived about the end of the second century.

Add to these three testimonies a catalogue which bears the name of Muratori, its discoverer, and which enumerates the books of the New Testament which from the first were considered canonical and sacred. The catalogue was written a little after the age of Pius I (A.D. 142–157), about A.D. 170, and probably in Rome itself; and at the head of the list it places our four Gospels. It is true that the first lines of this fragment, which refer to Matthew and Mark, have mostly perished, but immediately after the blank the name of Luke appears as the *third,* and that of John as the *fourth* ; so that, even in this remote age, we find even the order in which our Evangelists follow each other thus early attested to—Matthew, Mark, Luke, and John.

Let us quote two other witnesses, one of whom carries us back to an antiquity even more remote. We here refer to the two most ancient versions made of the New Testament. One of these translations is into Syriac, and is called the Peschitto. The other, in Latin, is known by the name of the Italic, and both assign the first place to the four Evangelists. The canonical authority of these four Gospel narratives must have been completely recognized and established in the mother Church before they would have been translated into the dialect of the daughter Churches, Syriac and Latin.

When are we to say that this took place? The Syriac version, which carries us as far East as to the banks of the Euphrates, is generally assigned to the end of the second century, and not without good reasons, though we have not any positive proof to offer. The Latin version had acquired, even before this period, a certain public authority. Thus the Latin translator of the great work of Irenæus, written in Greek, which we assign to the end of the second century (Tertullian, in fact, copies this translator in the quotation which he makes from Irenæus), and Tertullian also, at the end of the same century, follow the Italic version. The estimation in which the Latin version of the Gospels was then held, necessarily supposes that this translation must have been made some ten or twenty years at least before this. It is thus a well-established fact that already between A.D. 150 and 200, not only were the Gospels translated into Latin and Syriac, but also that their number was defined to be four only, neither more nor less ; and this remarkable fact is well calculated to throw light on the question of their true age and origin. We shall return to this farther on.

Let us pause here to consider again these two great Church teachers—Irenæus and Tertullian. Their testimony is decisive, and no one, even among those who deny the authenticity of St. John, is able to question it. We have here only to inquire whether their testimony is to be limited to the time only when they wrote—that is to say, whether it proves nothing more than the high consideration in which the Evangelists were held at the time when they wrote. In his refutation of these false teachers, Irenæus not only refers to the four Gospels with perfect confidence, and with the most literal exactness, but he even remarks that there are necessarily four, neither more nor less ; and in proof of this he adduces comparisons from the four quarters of the world, the four principal winds, and the four figures of the cherubim. He says that the four Evangelists are the four columns of the Church, which is extended over the whole world, and sees in this number four a peculiar appointment of the Creator of the world. I ask, then, is such a statement consistent with the assertion that the four Gospels first became of authority about the time of Irenæus, and that Christians then set up a fourth and a later Gospel, that of St. John, besides the other three older Gospels? Are we not rather constrained to admit that their authority was already then ancient and established, and that their number four was a matter already so undisputed that the Bishop Irenæus could justify and explain it in his own peculiar way, as we have just now seen? Irenæus died in the second year of the third century, but in his youth he had sat at the feet of the aged Polycarp, and Polycarp, in his turn, had been a disciple of the Evangelist St. John, and had conversed with other eye-witnesses of the Gospel narrative. Irenæus, in speaking of his own personal recollections, gives us Polycarp's own account of that which he had heard from the lips of St. John and other disciples of our Lord, and expressly adds that all these words agree with Scripture. But let us hear his own words, as contained in a letter to Florinus :—

" When I was yet a child I saw thee at Smyrna, in Asia Minor, at Polycarp's house, where thou wert distinguished at Court, and obtained the regard of the bishop. I can more distinctly recollect things which happened then than others more recent ; for events which happened in infancy seem to grow with the mind and to become part of ourselves, so that I can recall the very place where Polycarp used to sit and teach, his manner of speech, his mode of life, his appearance, the style of his address to the people, his frequent references to St. John and to others who had seen our Lord ; how he used to repeat from memory their discourses, which he had heard from them concerning our Lord, His miracles and mode of teaching, and how, being instructed himself by those who were eye-witnesses to the Word, there was in all that he said a strict agreement with the Scriptures."

This is the account which Irenæus himself gives of

his connection with Polycarp, and of the truths which
he had learned from him. Who will now venture to
question whether this Father had ever heard a word
from Polycarp about the Gospel of St. John? The
time when Irenæus, then a young man, was known
to Polycarp, who died a martyr at Smyrna, about
A.D. 165, could not have been later than A.D. 150 ;
yet they would have us believe that Irenæus had not
then heard a word from his master, Polycarp, about
the Gospel of St. John, though he so often recalled the
discourses of this apostle ! Any testimony of Polycarp
in favour of the Gospel refers us back to the Evangelist
himself ; for Polycarp, in speaking to Irenæus of this
Gospel as a work of his master, St. John, must have
learned from the lips of the Apostle himself whether
he was its author or not. There is nothing more
damaging to these doubters of the authenticity of St.
John's Gospel than this testimony of Polycarp ; and
there is no getting rid of this difficulty, unless by
setting aside the genuineness of the testimony itself.
This fact also becomes more striking if we consider it
under another aspect. What I mean is this : those
who deny the authenticity of St. John's Gospel, say
that this Gospel only appeared about A.D. 150, and
that Polycarp never mentioned the Gospel as such to
Irenæus. But in this case can we suppose that Irenæus
would have believed in the authenticity of this Gospel,
a work that professed to be the most precious legacy
of St. John to the Christian Church, as the narrative of
an eye-witness and an intimate friend of the Redeemer,
and a Gospel whose independent character, as regards
the other three, seemed to take away something from
their authority? The very fact that such a work of
St. John had never once been mentioned to him by
Polycarp would have at once convinced Irenæus that
it was an audacious imposture. And are we to believe

that Irenæus would produce such a forgery as this with which to reply to these false teachers, who themselves falsified Scripture, and appealed to apocryphal writings as if they were genuine and inspired! And are we further to suppose that he would have linked such a writing up with the other three Gospels to combine what he calls a quadruple or four-sided Gospel! What a tissue of contradictions, or rather, to use the right word, of absurdities!

These arguments, as we have just stated them, are not new ; they are at least found in Irenæus. They have been stated before, but they have scarcely ever received the consideration which they deserve. For our part, we think serious and reflecting men quite right in attaching more weight to these historic proofs of Irenæus, derived from Polycarp, in favour of the authenticity of St. John's Gospel, than to those scruples and negations of learned men of our day, who are smitten with a strange passion for doubt.

We say as much for Tertullian and his testimony. This man, who from an advocate of paganism became a powerful defender of the Christian truth, takes such a scrupulous view of the origin and worth of the four Evangelists that he will allow to Mark and Luke, as apostolic men, *i.e.* as companions and assistants of the apostles, only a certain subordinate place, while he upholds the full authority of John and of Matthew, on account of their character of real apostles, chosen by the Lord Himself. In his work against Marcion (book iv, chap. v), Tertullian lays down the principle by which we should decide on the truth of the articles of the Christian faith, and especially of that most important one of all, the authenticity of the apostolic writings. For this, he makes the value of a testimony to depend on its antiquity, and decides that we are to hold that to be true for us which was held to be true in former ages. This appeal to antiquity leads us back to the apostles' day, and in deciding what is the authenticity of any writing which claims to be apostolic, we must refer to those churches which were planted by the apostles. I ask, then, is it credible in any degree that this man, so sagacious, could have acted hastily and uncritically in accepting the credibility and authenticity of the four Evangelists? The passages I have referred to are taken from his celebrated reply to Marcion, who, on his own authority and in conformity with his own heretical tastes, had attacked the sacred text. Of the four Gospels, Marcion had completely rejected three, and the other, that of St. Luke, he had modified and mutilated according to his own caprice. Tertullian, in his reply, formally appeals to the testimony of the apostolic churches in favour of the four Gospels. Is such a challenge as this, in the mouth of such a man as Tertullian, to be passed by as of no weight? When he wrote his reply to Marcion, the apostle St. John had been dead only about a century. The Church of Ephesus, among whom the apostle St. John had so long lived, and in which city he died, had surely time to decide the question once for all, whether the Gospel of St. John was authentic or not. It was not difficult to find out what was the judgment of the apostolic Church on this question. Moreover, we must not forget that in Tertullian we have not merely a man of erudition, occupied in laying down learned theses, but a man of serious mind, to whom a question like this was one on which his faith, and with it the salvation of his soul, depended. Is it then likely that such a man would have given easy credence to writings like these, which concern the fundamental doctrines of Christianity— writings which distinctly claimed to be apostolic, and at which the wisdom of the world in which he had been educated professed to be offended? Now, since Tertullian expressly asserts, that in defending the apostolic origin of the four Evangelists he rests his case upon the testimony of the apostolic churches, we must be incorrigible sceptics to doubt any longer that he had not thoroughly examined for himself into the origin of these Gospels.

We maintain, then, that the attestations of Irenæus and Tertullian have a weight and a worth beyond the mere range of their own age. These attestations carry us up to the four first witnesses, and the evidence which they depose is in favour of these primitive times. This is the conclusion which we think we are warranted in drawing; and it is best established, not only by those more ancient witnesses above referred to and given by the writer of the list of books in the New Testament known as the Muratori catalogue, as well as the author of the Italic version, but also by the consent of the Church and the uncontradicted records of the earliest times prior to those of Irenæus and Tertullian.

My reader has doubtless heard of those works called *Harmonies of the Gospels*, in which the four narratives are moulded and fused into one. They sought in this way to produce a complete picture of our Lord's life, by supplementing the narrative of the one Gospel by details supplied from another, and especially by interpolating the discourses of St. John between those of the other Evangelists, so as to trace out in this way, step by step, the three years of the Lord's ministry. As early as A.D. 170, two learned men undertook works of this kind. One of these was Theophilus, Bishop of Antioch, in Syria; and the other Tatian, a disciple of the great divine and martyr, Justin. These two books are lost; but Jerome, in the fourth century, gives us some account of that of Theophilus, which he calls a combination of the four Gospels into one ; and Eusebius and Theodoret, in the fourth and fifth centuries, speak of that of Tatian in the same way. Tatian had given his the name of *Diatessaron*, that is, the Gospel according to Four. These two writers produced other works, which are still extant, and in which there are undoubted quotations from St. John's Gospel, not to speak of the other three. But these *Harmonies*, which have not come down to us, are of a much higher value than mere isolated quotations, and furnish a proof that at the time when they were first attempted the four Gospels were regarded as a single work, in which the variety of the narratives, which sometimes amounts to a real difference, was plainly perceptible. Hence a desire arose to draw out of these differences a higher unity, and combine them as one harmonious whole. These two attempts to write a " Harmony " were made soon after the middle of the second century, whence we may certainly conclude that the Gospels themselves were generally recognized and received as such for at least a long time previous.

We here pass by other testimonies, in order to say a few words on the letters of Ignatius and Polycarp, the disciples of the apostle, which carry us up to an age as early as the beginning of the second century. When the holy Ignatius, whom his master, St. John, had consecrated Bishop of Antioch, was led as a martyr to Rome, between A.D. 107 and A.D. 115, he wrote several letters while on his journey to Rome, of which we have two recensions, one shorter and the other longer. We shall here refer only to the shorter, which is enough for our purpose, since its genuineness is now generally admitted. These letters contain several passages drawn more or less directly from St. Matthew and St. John. Ignatius thus writes in his letter to the Romans :—

47

" I desire the bread of God, the bread of heaven, the bread of life, which is the flesh of Jesus Christ, the Son of God. And I desire the drink of God, the blood of Jesus Christ, who is undying love and eternal life." These words recall the sixth chapter of St. John, where it is said, " I am the bread which came down from heaven. I am the bread of life. I am the living bread. The bread that I shall give is My flesh. He that eateth My flesh and drinketh My blood hath eternal life " (verses 41, 48, 54).

In the same letter Ignatius writes, " What would a man be profited, if he should gain the whole world, and lose his own soul ? "—words literally found in Matthew xvi. 26.

Let us quote another passage of his letter to the Church of Smyrna, where it is said of Jesus that He was baptized by John, in order that He might fulfil all righteousness, and which exactly recalls Matthew iii. 15.

The short letter of Polycarp, written a little after the death of Ignatius, about A.D. 115, bears reference, in the same way, to certain passages of St. Matthew. So when we read, " We desire to pray to God, who sees all, that He may not lead us into temptation, for the Lord has said, that the spirit is willing, but the flesh is weak " (see Matt. vi. 13, and xxvi. 41).

Though we do not wish to give to the above references a decisive value, and though they do not exclude all doubt as to their applicability to our Gospels, and more particularly to that of St. John, they nevertheless undoubtedly bear traces of such a reference : and we have thus an additional proof to offer that our Gospels were in use at the commencement of the second century.

It is certainly a fact well deserving of attention that we find in the Epistle of Polycarp a certain trace of the use of the First Epistle of St. John. Polycarp writes thus : "Whosoever confesses not that Jesus Christ is come in the flesh is Antichrist." Now we read these words in the First Epistle of St. John iv. 3 : "Every spirit that confesses not that Jesus Christ is come in the flesh is not of God : and this is that spirit of Antichrist."

This passage of the Epistle of John, as cited by Polycarp, about A.D. 115, is of very great importance, since, in fact, the ideas and style in this Epistle and in the Gospel of St. John are so like, that we are compelled to refer them to the same writer. To recognize the Epistle, we must also recognize the Gospel. The testimony of Polycarp, if we bear in mind the close relationship in which he stood to the apostle, is, as we have seen above, of such weight that there is no room left to contradict or attack the authenticity of writings supported in this way. To get rid of this testimony, writers of the sceptical school have made use of the following argument : " It is not absolutely necessary to take these words of Polycarp as a quotation from St. John. They may have been sentiments which were current in the Church, and which John may have gathered up, as well as Polycarp, without pretending to have first originated them." A partisan of this school has had recourse to another means to evade the difficulty : " Can we not reverse the argument, and say that it is the author of the so-called Epistles of St. John who quotes Polycarp ? " A man must have some courage to start such an extravagant theory as this. But there are learned men capable even of this. And even if this does not succeed, they have one expedient yet, which they do not fail to use as the last resort of all. They will say that the letter is not Polycarp's at all. It is true that Irenæus, his disciple, believed in its genuineness : but what matters that? One has always some good reasons with which to back up an audacious assertion, and to shake and overthrow, if possible, a truth which is firmly established. I cannot, however, help saying to any one who shudders at these anti-Christian attempts, that they are as weak as they are worthless, and my reader will soon see that it is so.

Let us now turn to one of the most worthy of Polycarp's contemporaries—I refer to Justin Martyr, who already had been highly esteemed as a writer, before his martyrdom in Rome (about A.D. 166) had made his memory precious to the Church. Two of his works are taken up with a defence of Christianity. He presented these apologies to the Emperor, the first in A.D. 139; the second in A.D. 161. One can easily see from these dates, and especially from the earlier of the two, that it is important to know whether Justin supports the use and authority of our Gospels. It is well established that he has made use of the first three —that of Matthew in particular; and this fact is beyond the reach of the attacks of doubt. This is the very reason why sceptics say all the more obstinately that he does not make use of St. John. We, on the contrary, without hesitation, assert the very opposite. In several passages of Justin, we cannot fail to recognize an echo of that special sentence of St. John: "The Word was made flesh." The reply which Justin puts in the mouth of John the Baptist, when interrogated by the messenger of the Sanhedrin, "I am not the Christ, but the voice of one crying," is nothing but a citation of a passage of St. John i. 20–23. The apostle cites the words of Zechariah (chap. xii. 10) in such a way as they are found nowhere else; and as Justin uses the quotation in the same way, it is clear that he has borrowed them from St. John.

We also read in Justin's first Apology, A.D. 139,

" Christ has said, Except ye are born again, ye cannot enter into the kingdom of God ; but that it is impossible that those who are once born should enter a second time into their mother's womb and be born is clear to every one." There has been much dispute as to the meaning of this passage. For our part, we take the view that Justin was referring to John iii. 3-5, and to our Lord's discourse with Nicodemus : " Verily, verily, I say unto you, Except a man be born again, he cannot see the kingdom of God." That this passage of St. John occurred to Justin's mind is, in my judgment, indubitable on this account : that he adds in the same loose way in which he is in the habit of quoting the Old Testament, certain other words of our Lord, which, in the text of St. John, are as follows : " How can a man be born when he is old ? can he enter a second time into his mother's womb and be born ? " If we are justified in assuming the use of the Gospel of St. John by Justin, then the supposition that the Gospel was only written about A.D. 150, and is consequently unauthentic, is proved to be unwarranted.

We can also show in other ways that Justin proves that the authenticity of this Gospel was well established in his day. We will only refer to *one*. He tells us in the same Apology, written A.D. 139, that " The Memoirs of the Apostles or the writings of the Prophets are read, as long as time permits " (1 Apol. 67), every Lord's day in the assemblies of the Christians. Here we have to remark that the Gospels are placed side by side with the prophets. This undoubtedly places the Gospels in the rank of canonical books, the same as the prophets were regarded in the Jewish synagogue. But who in the world would ever think that the Church in the time of Justin used any other Gospels than those which we now know of, and which, within a few years of that time, were heard of throughout the whole Christian world? Indeed, it contradicts all that we know of the rise and origin of the Canon to suppose that as late as Justin Martyr's time, only Matthew, Mark, and Luke had been accepted as canonical, and that John's Gospel was brought in afterwards!

CHAPTER II

Our observations so far have been confined almost entirely to the writings of those men whom the Church of the second century regarded as pillars of the faith. During the same period, however, there sprang up a literature of heretical and erroneous teachers, which, like grafts of a wild tree, threw up a rank luxuriance of strange doctrine. We can produce satisfactory testimony even from writings of this kind, that about the middle, and before the middle, of the second century, our Gospels were held in the highest esteem by the Church. This branch of our inquiry is as interesting on account of the insight it gives us into the opinions of those erroneous teachers, as it is important on account of the information it gives us on the age and authority of our Gospels. In appealing to these false teachers as testimony to the truth of the Gospels, we follow no less a precedent than that of Irenæus, the well-known Bishop of Lyons, to whom we have already referred. Irenæus makes the observation : " So well established are our Gospels that even teachers of error themselves bear testimony to them : even they rest their objections on the foundation of the Gospels " (*Adv. Hær.* iii. 11, 7).

This is the judgment which the last half of the second century passes on the first half ; and this first half of the second century is the very time from which the opponents of the Gospel narrative draw their principal objections. Now, surely a man like Irenæus, who lived only twenty years or so later than this very

53

time, must have known this fact better than certain professors of the nineteenth century? The more respect, then, that we pay to the real culture and progress of our age, the less can we esteem those learned men who only use their knowledge and acuteness to make away with history. What Irenæus affirms is fully borne out by facts. We may, therefore, with all confidence intrust ourselves to his guidance. As a fact, the replies of the early Church fathers to these heretics, to which we owe all that we know about them, furnish positive proof that these false teachers admitted our Gospels to be, as the Church already declared them to be, canonical; and Irenæus, this Bishop of Lyons, is one of the chief authorities on this subject. Next to him we should place a work discovered about twenty years ago, of a disciple of Irenæus, by name Hippolytus, a man who lived sufficiently near the time of these erroneous teachers to be, like his master, a competent testimony on such a subject.

One of the most intelligent and able of these early heretics was Valentinus, who came from Egypt to Rome in the early part of the second century, and lived there about twenty years. He undertook to write a complete history of all the celestial evolutions which in the mysterious region of those celestial forces and heavenly intelligences (which he called the Pleroma) prepared the way for the coming of the Only-Begotten Son, and pretended to determine in this way the nature and power of that Only-Begotten Son. In this extravagant attempt he did not hesitate to borrow a number of expressions and ideas—such as the Word, the Only-Begotten, Life, Light, Fullness, Truth, Grace, the Redeemer, the Comforter—from the Gospel of St. John, and to use them for his own purposes. There is thus such an undeniable connection between the Gospel of St. John and this Valentinian scheme of doctrine that one of two explanations only is possible. Either Valentinus has borrowed from St. John, or St. John from Valentinus. After what we have said already, the latter supposition must appear utterly incredible, and a nearer consideration of the subject only confirms this. Now, when a sceptical school of our age resorts to such a hypothesis as this, it proclaims its own downfall. Irenæus, in fact, expressly declares that the Valentinians made fullest use of St. John's Gospel, and he shows us in detail how they drew from the first chapter some of their principal dogmas.

Hippolytus confirms this assertion of Irenæus. He quotes several of the sayings of our Lord as recorded by St. John, which were adopted by Valentinus. One of the most distinct references is that to John x. 8, of which Hippolytus writes : " Since the prophets and the law, according to Valentinus' doctrine, were marked by an inferior and less intelligent spirit, Valentinus says, ' Therefore, saith the Redeemer, All that ever came before Me were thieves and robbers ' " (Hippolytus, *Philosophoumenon*, vi. 35). It is easy to prove that Valentinus treated the other Gospels in the same way as he did that of St. John. According to Irenæus, he supposed that the inferior spirit, whom he called the Demiurge, or maker of the world, was typified in the centurion of Capernaum (Matt. viii. 9 ; Luke vii. 8). In the daughter of Jairus, dead and raised to life, he fancied a type of his lower wisdom (Achamoth), the mother of the Demiurge ; and in the history of the woman who for twelve years had the issue of blood, and who was healed by the Lord (Matt. ix. 20), he saw a figure of the suffering and deliverance of his twelfth Æon.

What bearing, then, has all this on our inquiry?

Already, before the middle of the second century, we see that our Gospels, and especially that of St. John, were held in such esteem that even a fantastic philosopher attempted to find support in the simple words of the Gospels for his fanciful scheme of celestial Powers, primitive Intelligences, Æons, and so forth.

Besides Valentinus, we possess a learned letter written by a disciple of his, by name Ptolemy. It contains, in addition to several quotations from St. Matthew, a passage taken from the first chapter of St. John, in these words : " The apostle says that all things were made by Him, and that without Him was not anything made that was made."

Another distinguished follower and companion of Valentinus, by name Heracleon, wrote an entire commentary on the Gospel of St. John, several fragments of which still remain. In it he endeavours to twist the words of the Gospel into agreement with the fancies of Valentinus. What must have been the esteem, then, in which this Gospel was held in the second century, when a leading follower of such a fanciful and erroneous theorist as Valentinus should feel himself driven to draw up a commentary on this Gospel, in order to make it support his heresy !

Valentinus and his school were not the only writers who sought, though hostile to the Church, to have the Gospels on their side instead of against them. There were other sects, such as the Naassenes, so called from their possessing the spirit of the serpent (Nachash) that tempted our first parents, and the Peratici, a sect of enthusiasts, so called from their pretending to see into the heavenly future, who wove into their teaching many passages of St. John, as we learn from Hippolytus.

Already under Adrian, between A.D. 117 and 138, Basilides had written a long work to explain the

Gospels in the same fantastic spirit as Valentinus. We can only infer this from a few fragments which remain to us. But we can say, with some degree of certainty, that he used the Gospel of St. John ; for Hippolytus expressly says that he used the expressions, " That was the true light which lighteth every man that cometh into the world " (John i. 9), and " Mine hour is not yet come " (John ii. 4).

Let us not pass over another heretic of the early part of the second century, whose name has been used by those who take the contrary view. We refer to Marcion, in reply to whom Tertullian wrote the work we have above referred to. He was born at Sinope, on the shores of the Black Sea ; but it was at Rome that he afterwards wrote those works which brought his name into notice. It was his special effort to break the link which connects Christianity with Judaism, and for this reason he tried to get rid of everything in the apostles' teaching which seemed to countenance Judaism. As we learn from Church history that Marcion composed a canon of Scripture adapted to his own peculiar views, and that this collection contained only the Gospel of St. Luke, with ten of the Apostle Paul's Epistles, and that he even accommodated the text of these to fit in with his notions, certain learned men have thought that this was the first collection of Holy Scripture known to the Church —that his Gospel was the original of that which now passes for the Gospel of St. Luke, and that he was not acquainted with the Gospel of St. John. We hold that all these three assertions are quite erroneous : as regards the second of the three, it is admitted on all sides to be so. As to the third of these assumptions, of which so much has been made, that Marcion was unacquainted with St. John's Gospel, the following testimony of Tertullian is decisive against it. This

57

writer tells us of an earlier work of Marcion's, in which he made use of all the four Gospels, and that to suit his own purposes he afterwards rejected all but that of St. Luke. We have not the least right to doubt this statement, since the whole of Tertullian's reply to Marcion rests on this point as on an undisputed fact.

These heretics, then, of the early Church have rendered considerable service by their testimony to the early reception of the Gospels. We now pass them by to notice those open enemies of Christianity, to whom the preaching of the Cross was nothing but a stumbling-block and foolishness. About the middle of the second century there was such an one in Celsus, who wrote a book full of ridicule and reproach against Christianity. The book itself has long since been lost —a fate which it well deserved ; and yet, in spite of all its bitterness and scorn, it did no real damage to the young Christian Church still suffering under per-secution—a fact which is encouraging to us, who have to meet similar attacks in the present day. It is well for us, however, that Origen has preserved several extracts from this book of Celsus. From these extracts we gather that Celsus, in attacking Christianity, made use of the Gospels, and, as " the writings of the disciples of Jesus," employed them to show what was believed by Christians. He notices in this way the story of the wise men coming from the East, the flight of the child Jesus into Egypt, the appearing of the dove at our Lord's baptism, His birth from a virgin, His agony in the garden, His thirst on the cross, etc. While he gathers these facts from the first three Gospels, he takes even more details from the Gospel of St. John ; as, for example, that Jesus was asked by the Jews in the Temple to do some miracle, that Jesus was known as the Word of God, that at the crucifixion blood flowed from His side. Of the accounts of the resurrection he notices that in one Gospel there are two angels, and in another Gospel only one is spoken of as present at the grave ; to which Origen said, in reply, that the one account is based on the Gospels of St. Luke and St. John, the other on that of St. Matthew and St. Mark. We may, therefore, conclude that this heathen opponent of the Gospel in the second century knew of the four Gospels which we possess, and considered them, as we do, to be genuine apostolic writings.

CHAPTER III

APOCRYPHAL LITERATURE

THE same service which the early heretics and heathen opponents of Christianity render to our cause, we may get from consulting the so-called Apocrypha of the New Testament. My reader will ask, What is this Apocryphal literature? Now I can give some information on this subject, as I have paid much attention to it, and have discovered several originals in old libraries, and edited them for the first time. In 1848 I wrote an essay, which obtained a prize in Holland, on the origin and worth of the Apocryphal Gospels. The Apocryphal books are writings composed with a view of being taken up into the Canon, and put on a level with the inspired books, but which were deliberately rejected by the Church. They bear on their front the names of apostles, or other eminent men ; but have no right to do so. These names were used by obscure writers to palm off their productions. But for what purpose were these Apocryphal books written? Partly to embellish and add to, in some fanciful way of their own, Scripture narratives ; partly to invent others about the Saviour, Mary, Joseph, and the apostles ; and partly to support false doctrines, for which there was no support in Scripture. As these objects were decidedly pernicious, the Church was fully justified in rejecting these writings. They nevertheless contain much that is interesting and curious, and in early times, when the Church was not so critical in distinguishing the true from the false, they were given a place which they did not deserve. We have already explained in what sense we shall use them :

they will go to strengthen our proof for the early reception of the canonical Gospels. Everything will therefore depend upon the age of these Apocryphal writings, and here we confine ourselves to two only —the Gospel of St. James, and the so-called Acts of Pilate. We think we shall be able to prove that both of these date from the early part of the second century. To begin with the Gospel of James.

In Justin Martyr's Apology, written A.D. 139, we find certain details of the birth of our Lord, which are only found in this so-called Gospel of St. James. Justin relates that the birth of Christ was in a grotto near Bethlehem ; so we read in the Apocryphal Gospel. In the account of the Annunciation to the Virgin Mary, Justin concludes with the words, " And thou shalt call His name Jesus " ; and he adds, immediately after, " for He shall save His people from their sins." The order is the same in St. James's Gospel. According to St. Matthew, these words were spoken to Joseph ; while they are wholly wanting in St. Luke's Gospel. We pass by other instances. But an objection may be raised. It may be said that Justin obtained this account from some other document since lost. For my part, I cannot agree with this objection. I find no references to any lost Gospels ; the attempts to discover them on the part of the sceptical school have not been successful ; and as the materials of Justin's information lie before us in the Gospel of St. James, I have no hesitation in ascribing it to that source. Not only does Origen mention this Gospel of St. James as everywhere known about the end of the second century, but we have also about fifty manuscripts of his Gospel of the date of the ninth century, and also a Syriac of the sixth century. To get rid of the inference that Justin made use of this Gospel, we must lose ourselves in wild conjecture.

Now the whole of the writing called after St. James is so closely related to our Gospels, that they must have been extensively known and used before the former was concocted. Matthew and Luke had declared that Mary was a virgin-mother : now there were sects who taught that there was also a son naturally born to Joseph and Mary ; that the brethren of Jesus are referred to in the Gospels seems to imply this. There were learned Jews who denied the meaning of the prophet's reference to the Virgin (Matt. i. 23), and heathen and Jews as well mocked at the doctrine of a son born to a virgin. These objections were raised as early as the former part of the second century, and the Gospel of St. James was written in reply to these objections. It set forth by proving that from her birth Mary had been highly favoured, that from her birth she was marked out as the Virgin, and that her relationship to Joseph always stood higher than that of a mere matrimonial union. Now if this writing is assigned to the early part of the second century, the Gospels of St. Matthew and St. Luke, on which it is grounded, could not have been written later than the end of the first century.

It is the same with the Acts of Pilate,[1] with this difference only—that it rests on the Gospel of St. John as well as on the other Evangelists. Justin is our earliest authority for a writing which professed to have appeared under Pilate, and which adduces fresh and convincing testimony for the Godhead of Christ from

[1] Tischendorf stands almost alone amongst scholars in his views as to the authenticity of the Acts of Pilate, so called. That some official report was made to the Emperor by the governor is, indeed, highly probable. That this document became known to the early Christians, and was quoted by Justin and Tertullian, may likewise be conceded. But few, if any, modern scholars are prepared to accept Tischendorf's conclusion that the modern volume represents the original document.

events before, during, and after His crucifixion. That
it was a pious fraud of some Christian, neither Justin,
Tertullian, nor any other ever suspected. On the contrary, Justin twice refers to it. First, he refers to it in
connection with the prophecies of the crucifixion (Isa.
lxv. 2 ; lviii. 2 ; Ps. xxii. 16–18), adding, " That this
really took place, you can see from the Acts composed
under Pontius Pilate " ; and in the second place, when
he adduces the miraculous cures wrought by Christ,
and predicted by Isaiah (Isa. xxxv. 4–6), he adds,
" That Jesus did these things, you may see in the Acts
of Pontius Pilate." The testimony of Tertullian is even
more express (*Apology*, xxi.) when he says, " The doctors
of the law delivered Jesus, through envy, to Pilate ;
that Pilate, yielding to the clamour of His accusers,
gave Him up to be crucified ; that Jesus, in yielding
up His breath on the cross, uttered a great cry, and at
the instant, at mid-day, the sun was darkened ; that
a guard of soldiers was set at the tomb, to keep the
disciples from taking away the body, for He had fore-
told His resurrection ; that on the third day the earth
suddenly shook, and that the stone before the sepulchre
was rolled away, and that they found only the grave-
clothes in the tomb ; that the chief men in the nation
spread the report that His disciples had taken away
the body, but that Jesus spent forty days still in Galilee,
instructing His apostles, and that, after giving them the
command to preach the Gospel, He was taken up to
heaven in a cloud." Tertullian closes this account
with the words, " Pilate, urged by his conscience to
become a Christian, reported these things to Tiberius,
who was then emperor."

These are the testimonies of Justin and Tertullian
as to the Acts of Pilate. We have to this day several
ancient Greek and Latin manuscripts of a work
which corresponds with these citations, and which

bears the same name as that referred to by Justin. Is it, then, the same which Justin and Tertullian had read?

This view of the question has been opposed in several ways. Some have maintained that these testimonies only existed in imagination, but that the writing itself, suggested by these very quotations, afterwards appeared. But this is a baseless supposition. Others think that the original has been lost, and that these are only copies of it. Is there any ground for supposing this? No. It is true that the original text has been altered in many places; and in the Middle Ages the Latins mixed up the title of the Acts of Pilate with that of the Acts of Nicodemus, and added a preface to it in this altered form; and lastly, side by side with the ancient Greek text, we have a recast of it comparatively modern. But, notwithstanding all this, there are decisive reasons for maintaining that the Acts of Pilate, now extant, contain substantially that which Justin and Tertullian had before them. Our own researches in the great libraries of Europe have led us to discover important documents to prove this. I would mention only an Egyptian manuscript, or papyrus, and a Latin manuscript, both of the fifth century. This last, though rubbed over about a thousand years ago, and written over with a new writing, is still legible by practised eyes (manuscripts of this kind are called palimpsests). These two originals—one Egyptian, the other Latin—confirm the high antiquity of our Greek text, on which they were founded; for, if there were versions of these Acts as early as the fifth century, the original itself must certainly be older.

Let us look at the matter a little more closely. This ancient work was very highly prized by the Christians. Justin and Tertullian are proofs of this, and Justin even appeals to it, in writing to an emperor, as to a decisive testimony. It still maintained its place of authority, as Eusebius and Epiphanius attest. The first tells us that at the beginning of the fourth century the Emperor Maximian, who was hostile to Christianity, caused some pretended Acts of Pilate to be published, full of false charges and calumnies, and circulated it through the schools with the evident intention of throwing into the shade and discrediting the Acts which the Christians prized so highly. I ask, then, is it the least credible that this ancient Apocryphal book, so freely used up to this time, could have been so completely recast towards the end of the fourth or fifth century as that the original disappeared, and a spurious version took its place? Such a supposition violates all probability, and also carries a contradiction on the face of it, in that it implies that a work so mutilated could retain at the same time a certain real resemblance to the Gospels. Such a theory can only mislead those who are entirely ignorant of the subject. We cannot class ourselves among such : we rather rely with confidence on our own conscientious examination of the documents, and our conclusion is as follows. Our Acts of Pilate not only presuppose acquaintance with the first three Gospels, but also and especially with St. John's. For if the details of the crucifixion and resurrection rest on the former, those of the trial of Christ refer to the latter. It follows from all this that as the so-called Acts of Pilate must have been compiled about the beginning of the second century (as Justin, A.D. 139, refers to them), the original Gospels on which they are based, including that of St. John, must have been written in the first century.

This conclusion is so satisfactory and decisive, that we do not seek to add anything to it from any further uses of the Apocryphal books of the New Testament.

CHAPTER IV

THE testimony of the Acts of Pilate and the Book of
James falls thus within the early part of the second
century. We have advanced step by step from the
latter to the former part of this century. Another
remarkable writing of this age here meets us at this
time—a writing which was put together by several
remarkable men between the end of the second and the
beginning of the fourth century. That it bears most
decisively on the question of the authorship of the
Gospels we can now most confidently maintain since
the discovery of the Sinaitic Bible. We here speak of
the Epistle of Barnabas.

The Epistle, in its style and matter, resembles that
to the Hebrews. It is addressed to those Christians
who, coming out of Judaism, desired to retain, under
the New Testament, certain peculiarities of the Old—
in the same way that the Judaizing teachers among
the Galatians had acted. In opposition to such ten-
dencies the Epistle asserts the truth that the new
covenant which Christ established had abolished the
old, and that the old was never more than an imperfect
type and shadow of the new.

During the last two centuries this Epistle has been
well known ; but, unfortunately, the first four chapters
were wanting in the copies of all the Greek manuscripts
found in the libraries of Europe. It was only in a
Latin version, and that of a very corrupt text, that the
entire Epistle was to be read. In this Latin version
there was a passage, in the fourth chapter, which had

excited peculiar attention : " Let us take care that we be not of those of whom it is written—that many were called, but few chosen." The expression, " as it is written," every reader of the New Testament is familiar with already. I would ask you to read Matthew iv. 1–11, where the temptation of our Lord is recorded. The weapon which our Lord used against the tempter is contained in the words, " It is written " ; and even the tempter uses this weapon in return, plying his temptation with the words, " It is written." It is the formula by which expressions out of Scripture are distinguished from all others, and marked out as the Word of God written. The apostles, like the Saviour, often use the expression when introducing a quotation from the Old Testament. It was natural, therefore, to apply this form of expression to the apostles' writings, as soon as they had been placed in the Canon with the books of the Old Testament. When we find, therefore, in ancient ecclesiastical writings, quotations from the Gospels introduced with this formula, " It is written," we must infer that at the time when the expression was used the Gospels were certainly treated as of equal authority with the books of the Old Testament. As soon as they were thus placed side by side, there was a Canon of the New Testament as well as of the Old, for the words which are referred to under the formula in Barnabas' Epistle are found, as is well known, in Matthew xxii. 14, and also xx. 16. If his argument is of any weight, it follows that, at the time when the Epistle of Barnabas was written, the Gospel of St. Matthew was treated as part of Holy Scripture.

But as the Epistle of Barnabas is undoubtedly of high antiquity, the fact that the formula, " It is written," is used, has been disputed by many learned men. And what gave some countenance to the doubt is this, that the first five chapters were extant only in the Latin version. They were able to say that this important expression was introduced by the Latin translator. A learned theologian, Dr. Credner, literally wrote, in the year 1832, as follows :—" This disputed expression does not exist for us in the original Greek. It would have been easy for the translator to introduce the usual formula, and for internal reasons we shall hold the genuineness of the phrase to be unproved till the contrary is proved." The decision, then, of the genuineness or not of the expression depended upon the discovery of the original Greek text. And not long after these words of Credner were written the original Greek text was discovered. While men were disputing in learned Germany as to whether the Latin version was to be relied on in this question or not, the original Greek text, which was to decide the question, lay hid in a Greek convent in the deserts of Arabia, among a heap of old parchments. While so much has been lost in the course of centuries by the tooth of time and the carelessness of ignorant monks, an invisible Eye had watched over this treasure, and when it was on the point of perishing in the fire, the Lord had decreed its deliverance. In the Sinaitic Bible, the entire of this Epistle of Barnabas has been found in the original Greek. And how does this original text decide this important question ? It decides that this expression, " It is written," was first prefixed to the quotation from St. Matthew, not by the Latin translator, but by the author himself in the Greek original.

Since this momentous fact has been decided in this unexpected way, it has been asked a second time, whether we are entitled to draw from it such important consequences. Might not the formula, " It is written," have been applied to any other written book ? That this could not be the case, our previous remarks on the use of the formula sufficiently prove. We have no right whatever to weaken the use of the expression in this particular case. But a critic of the negative school has tried to show his ingenuity in a peculiar way. In an Apocryphal book, called the Fourth Book of Ezra, written probably by some Jewish Christian, after the destruction of Jerusalem, we read : " For many are born, but few shall be saved." This expression has a certain resemblance to the expression of St. Matthew, but it is clearly different. But a learned man has, with all seriousness, attempted to show that the words of the Saviour, introduced by the expressive, " It is written," in the Epistle of Barnabas, are not really taken from St. Matthew, but from this Book of Ezra, and that the writer of the Epistle has substituted the one phrase for the other ; and consequently that the formula, " It is written," applies to the Apocryphal Book of Ezra, not to the Gospel of St. Matthew. It is characteristic of Strauss, who has attempted to turn the life of Jesus into a mere fancy or cloud picture, that he has marked with his approval this trick of conjuring away a passage in the Epistle of Barnabas. For our part, we see in it nothing more than an outcome of that anti-Christian spirit which has matured itself in the school of Renan. It is best described in the words of the apostle to Timothy (2 Tim. iv. 4), " And they shall turn away their ears from the truth, and shall be turned unto fables." I think the reader will now agree with me when I say, that so long as nothing stronger than this can be adduced to weaken the force of this passage in the Epistle of Barnabas, no one can go wrong who simply holds by the truth. The above effort of misapplied ingenuity only proves what efforts must be made to get rid of the force of the passage.

We have to consider these conclusions yet more

attentively. The Epistle of Barnabas does not date from later than the early part of the second century. While critics have generally been divided between assigning it to the first or second decade of the second century, the Sinaitic Bible, which has for the first time cleared up this question, has led us to throw its composition as far back as the last decade of the first century. In this venerable document there are several passages which refer to St. Matthew's Gospel (as in chapter ix. 13, when our Lord says, He was not come to call the righteous but sinners to repentance : the words "to repentance" are here introduced in the Epistle of Barnabas, as well as in St. Matthew's Gospel, by way of explanation, from Luke v. 32). It is very probable, also, that the remarks of Barnabas on the serpent of Moses as a type of the Saviour are founded on the well-known passage in John iii. 14. It is remarkable, more-over, that Matthew xxii. 14 is introduced with the usual formula which marks a quotation from Holy Scripture. It is clear, therefore, that at the beginning of the second century the Gospel of St. Matthew was already regarded as a canonical book.

This result is all the more remarkable when we consider that St. Matthew's Gospel has been considered not so much a book by itself, as one of four Gospels that together entered into the Canon of the New Testament. The inquiries which we have made into the first three quarters of the second century have given prominence at one time to the Gospel of St. Matthew, at another time to that of St. Luke and St. John ; but the Gospel of St. Mark has been less noticed, as it furnished fewer citations. It would not be fair to infer from this that the Gospel which was alone cited, alone had any authority in the early Church. Now the use which Justin makes of the Acts of Pilate proves to us that, at least as early as the end of the first century, the Gospel of

70

John must have been in use; and Justin himself, in the first half of the second century, makes frequent reference to St. John, and even more frequent to St. Matthew's Gospel. Is not this of itself a sufficient proof that if, at the time when Barnabas' Epistle was written, St. Matthew's Gospel was considered canonical, the same must be the case with St. John? Basilides, in the reign of Adrian (117–138) made use of St. John and St. Luke. Valentinus, about A.D. 140, makes use of St. Matthew, St. Luke, and St. John. Are not these additional proofs in our favour? Already as early as the time of Justin the expression, " the Evangel," was applied to the four Gospels, so that the name of each of the four writers dropped into the background ; and in the second half of the second century we find the number of the Evangelists restricted to four, and the matter treated as a subject which was beyond dispute. What follows from this? It follows that no one of these Gospels could have been elevated by itself to a place of authority in the Canon of Scripture. The Church only ventured to place them in the Canon when they had been already received as the four Gospels, and as such had been long prized as genuine apostolical writings.

When we further ask ourselves when this took place, we are forced to the conclusion that it must have occurred about the end of the first century. This was the time when, after the death of the aged John, those holy men who had known the Lord in the flesh, including the great Apostle of the Gentiles and the early Church, had thus lost a definite centre of authority. It was at this time, when the Church dispersed over the world, was persecuted without, and distracted by error within, that she began to venerate and regard as sacred the writings which the apostles had left behind them as precious depositories of truth, as unerring records of the life of the Saviour, and as an authoritative rule of faith and practice. The right time had therefore come for enrolling their writings among the Canon of Scripture. The separation between the Church and the Synagogue was now complete. Since the destruction of Jerusalem and the Temple service, A.D. 70, the Church had been thrown more entirely on her own resources, and stood now independent. It was a marked proof of her independence when she ventured to rank her sacred writings on a level with those of the Old Testament, which the Christian Church herself prized so highly.

Do you ask in what way and by what act was this done? Certainly no learned assemblies sat to decide this question. If men like Matthew, Mark, Luke, and John had left behind them outlines of the Lord's life, did it need anything more than their names to make their writings of the highest value to the early Church? And had not these men stood in such near relationship to the Church as to make it impossible to pass off forged writings of theirs without detection? There was no Gospel more difficult to be tampered with than St. John's. His Gospel went forth from the midst of the circle of Churches of Asia Minor, and spread thence into all the world. Was this possible if the slightest taint of suspicion had lain upon it? Suppose, on the other hand, that it first appeared elsewhere, then we may be sure that these Asiatic Churches would have been the first to detect the fraud. It would have been impossible to palm upon them a spurious document as the writing of their former bishop.

We have an old tradition on the subject, which Eusebius, in his Church History (iii. 24), has referred to. It says that the three Gospels already extensively known were laid before St. John by his friends. He bore witness to their truth, but said that they had passed over what Jesus had done at the beginning of His public ministry. His friends then expressed a desire that he should give an account of this period which had been passed over. This narrative is substantially confirmed by the contents of St. John's Gospel, a point which Eusebius has not failed to notice.

We conclude, then, that it was towards the end of the first century, and about the time of John's decease at Ephesus, that the Church began to place the four Gospels in the Canon. The reasons which lead us to assign this as the right date for the commencement of the Canon are of themselves sufficient ; but we would not so confidently maintain this opinion of the history and literature of the entire second century, as far as we have been able to look into the subject, did it not support our view of the case.

We have only one authority more to produce in our review of the earliest Christian literature. It is the testimony of Papias, who more than any other has been misrepresented by modern opponents of the Gospel. The uncertainty which rests over Papias himself and his testimony does not allow us to class him in the same rank with the other testimonies we have already adduced. But such as it is, we here produce it.

We learn from Eusebius (iii. 39) that Papias wrote a work in five books, which he called a *Collection of the Sayings of the Lord*. In collecting materials for this work, he preferred to lean rather on uncertain traditions than on what was written in books. He drew accordingly upon certain oral traditions which could be traced up to the apostles. His own words on these traditions are as follows : " I intend to put together what has been reported to me by the elders of that time, in so far as I have been able to verify it through my own enquiries." He adds further, "Whenever I met any one who had held converse with these elders, I at once enquired after the words of the elders, what Andrew, Peter, or Philip, or Thomas, James, or John, or Matthew, or any other of the Lord's disciples, had said." It is not clear from these words whom he means by the elders. Some learned men have erroneously supposed that he referred to the apostles themselves as his authorities. It is much more likely that he refers to those venerable men who had spoken with the apostles. So Eusebius thinks, who had the whole work of Papias before him, and he distinctly says so. He records of Papias that he nowhere claims to have seen or heard the holy apostles but as a pupil of Aristion and of John the Presbyter, to whose testimony he generally refers. It struck Eusebius, therefore, that it was an error in Irenæus to call Papias "a disciple of John and the companion of Polycarp," a mistake which he fell into by confounding John the Presbyter with the Apostle John. This is confirmed by the wonderful tradition which Irenæus relates of the millennial reign, "out of the mouth of those elders who had seen John, the Lord's disciple." In this place, Irenæus undoubtedly distinguishes between these elders and the apostles. But inasmuch as he appeals to Papias as his authority for this tradition of a reign of a thousand years, he leaves no doubt that the elders of whom he speaks are no others than those named by Papias.

Eusebius gives some further extracts from this work of Papias, namely, the story related to him by the daughters of Philip the Deacon, of the raising to life of a dead man by their father, and that Justus Barsabas had drunk a cup of poison without receiving any hurt. Papias went on further (we follow here the account of

74

Eusebius) to give some detailed accounts which he professed to have received by tradition, such as " certain unknown parables and lessons of our Lord and others, some of which are fabulous." Of this kind is the doctrine of a millennial kingdom, which is to take place in a certain carnal sense on this earth after the general resurrection. Eusebius has not given us a delineation of this kingdom, but Irenæus has. It is as follows : " The days shall come in which vines shall grow, of which each vine shall bear ten thousand branches, each branch ten thousand clusters, each cluster ten thousand grapes, and each grape contain ten measures of wine ; and when any one of the saints shall go to pluck a grape, another grape shall cry out, ' I am better ; take me, and praise the Lord.' So each corn of wheat shall produce ten thousand ears, and each ear ten thousand grains," etc.

This narrative Papias professed to have received from certain elders, who in their turn received it from St. John. Eusebius remarks on this, that Papias, who was a man of very narrow understanding, as his book fully proves, must have got these opinions from misunderstanding some of the apostle's writings. He goes on to say that there are other accounts of the Lord's sayings taken from Aristion and Presbyter John to be found in Papias' book, for which he refers the curious to the book itself. Here, Eusebius says, he will close his remarks on Papias with one tradition about St. Mark. It is to this effect : " And so the Presbyter said—Mark, the interpreter of Peter, had written down whatever saying of Peter's he could remember, but not the sayings and deeds of Christ in order ; for he was neither a follower of the Lord, nor had heard Him, but, as we have seen above, learned these things from Peter, who was in the habit of referring to the events of the Lord's life as occasion might suggest, but never in any systematic way. Mark, in consequence, never failed to write down these remembrances as they fell from Peter's lips, and was never known to have failed in thus preserving an exact record of what Peter said."

To these extracts from Papias, Eusebius added another upon St. Matthew, as follows : " Thus far on St. Mark—as to St. Matthew, Papias tells us that he wrote his words of the Lord in Hebrew, and whoever could do so afterwards translated it." In this extract there is something obscure ; it is doubtful whether we have rightly rendered " the words of the Lord," since what Papias has before observed upon Mark (we refer to the words, " What Christ has spoken or done ") makes it probable that we are to include under the expression both words and deeds. [Now, all these traditions of the Presbyter John and of Papias are derived from the Gospels of St. Matthew and St. Luke.] Even if the expression, " the words of the Lord," is to be understood strictly, we are not to conclude that there was then no written record of these sayings already in existence, since neither Eusebius nor any other early writer ever supposed that these extracts of Papias stood in contradiction with the two Gospels of Matthew and Mark. When, therefore, modern writers undertake to show that our Gospel of Mark is not the original Gospel written by St. Mark himself, but only a compilation from that original, this very theory convicts itself of being an arbitrary assumption. The theory is only too well adapted to invite a spirit of loose conjecture as to the origin of our Gospels.

This is true of St. Matthew's Gospel, as well as of St. Mark's. The point of the extract from Papias about St. Matthew lies in this, that he says that the Evangelist wrote it in Hebrew. If this assertion of

Papias is well founded, the next saying of his, "that any one translated it who was able to do so," opens a wide field for supposing all manner of differences between the Hebrew original and the Greek text. This Hebrew text must have been lost very early, as not one even of the very oldest Church Fathers had ever seen or used it. My reader will observe that I am casting a hasty glance at a very tangled and intricate question. For our part, we are fully satisfied that Papias' assertion of an original Hebrew text rests on a misunderstanding of his. To make this clear would take up too much space ; we can, therefore, only give here the following brief explanation of Papias' error.

From the Epistle of St. Paul to the Galatians, we gather that thus early there was a Judaizing party. This party spirit broke out even more fiercely after the destruction of Jerusalem. There were two parties among these Judaizers ; the one the Nazarenes, and the other the Ebionites. Each of these parties used a Gospel according to St. Matthew ; the one party using a Greek text, and the other party a Hebrew. That they did not scruple to tamper with the text to suit their creed is probable from that very sectarian spirit. The text, as we have certain means of proving, rested upon our received text of St. Matthew, with, however, occasional departures, to suit their arbitrary views. When, then, it was reported in later times that these Nazarenes, who were one of the earliest Christian sects, possessed a Hebrew version of Matthew, what was more natural than that some person or other thus falling in with the pretensions of this sect should say that Matthew originally was written in Hebrew, and that the Greek was only a version from it ? How far these two texts differed from each other no one cared to inquire ; and with such separatists as the

Nazarenes, who withdrew themselves to the shores of the Dead Sea, it would not have been easy to have attempted it.

Jerome supports us in this clearing up of Papias' meaning. Jerome, who knew Hebrew, as other Latin and Greek Fathers did not, obtained in the fourth century a copy of this Hebrew Gospel of the Nazarenes, and at once asserted that he had found the Hebrew original. But when he looked more closely into the matter, he confined himself to the statement that many supposed that this Hebrew text was the original of St. Matthew's Gospel. He translated it into Latin and Greek and added a few observations of his own on it. From these observations of Jerome, as well as from other fragments, we must conclude that this notion of Papias—in which several learned men of our day agree—that the Hebrew was the original text of St. Matthew, cannot be substantiated ; but, on the contrary, this Hebrew has been drawn from the Greek text, and disfigured moreover here and there with certain arbitrary changes. The same is applicable to a Greek text of the Hebrew Gospel in use among the Ebionites. This text, from the fact that it was in Greek, was better known to the Church than the Hebrew version of the Nazarenes ; but it was always regarded, from the earliest times, as only another text of St. Matthew's Gospel. This explains also what Papias had said about several translations of St. Matthew.

We have something more to say about Papias and his strange compilation. On the subject of his materials, he says that he sought for little help from written records. Of what records does he here speak? Is it of our Gospels? This is not impossible from the expression itself, but from the whole character of his book it seems very improbable, since it seems to have been his object to supplement these with traditions about the Saviour which were current about A.D. 130 or 140. We cannot suppose that the Gospels themselves were the storehouses from which he compiled these traditions. He must have sought for them among those Apocryphal writings which began to circulate from the very first. To those traditions of the Apocryphal Gospels he opposed his own collections of traditions, whose genuineness he pretended could, like the Gospels themselves, be traced up to the apostles.

We have seen already from Eusebius' notice of Papias' work, what kind of traditions they were which he collected—traditions such as those about Philip the Deacon having raised the dead, or Justus Barsabas having drunk poison without receiving any hurt. A third tradition of the same kind, which he says is contained in the Gospel of the Hebrews, is that of the history of a woman who was a sinner accused before Jesus. In this same book also, as we learn from Œcumenius, there is a story to the effect that the body of Judas the betrayer was so swollen, that being thrown down by a chariot in a narrow street, all his bowels gushed out. The book also contained, as we have already seen on the authority of Eusebius, certain unknown parables and lessons of our Lord ; but he does not think it worth his while to notice one of them ; nor did any other Church writer do so, with the exception of Irenæus (whose account of Papias' millenarian fancies we have already referred to) and Andrew of Cæsarea, in the sixth century, who notices, in his Commentary on the Book of Revelation, a remark of Papias about the fallen angels. Eusebius, for his part, dismisses these accounts of Papias, about parables of our Lord, which he received by tradition, as " altogether fabulous."

Now, with all that we thus know about the truth of Papias and his book, what credit are we to attach to him as a testimony for our Gospels? Though there are men of ability here and there who have credited Papias, we cannot help taking the contrary side. Eusebius' opinion about Papias, that he was a man of very contracted mind, is proved, not only by the extracts from him we have already noticed, but also by the way in which his attempt to enrich the Gospel narrative has been allowed to drop into oblivion by the entire Christian Church. How we should have prized even a single parable of our Lord, if it had borne any internal marks of being genuine! But no one paid the slightest attention to this collection of Papias ; the air of fable, which even Eusebius—who is himself by no means remarkable for critical acumen—exposes, throws a cloud of suspicion over the whole book.

Yet, notwithstanding all this, there are men in the present century, professing to be models of critical severity, who set up Papias as their torch-bearer in these inquiries. They have attempted to use his obscure and contradictory remarks about St. Matthew and St. Mark, to separate between the original element and the spurious additions to these Gospels. This is indeed to set up Papias on a pedestal! But Papias is even more readily seized on by those who wish to overturn the credit of St. John's Gospel. And why so? Papias is silent as to this Gospel. This silence of Papias is advanced by Strauss, Renan, and such-like opponents of the faith of the Church, as a most damaging fact against the genuineness of the Gospel. I rather think our readers who have measured Papias aright will not readily agree to this. Did not the motive betray itself, I would ask the reader, whether producing Papias as a witness on such a question does not imply a misunderstanding of him and his book? His notices about St. Matthew and St. Mark do not change the character of his book. But they say that Papias could not have known of John's Gospel, or he would have mentioned it. We have thus a proof that the Gospel could not have been in existence, since Papias was Bishop of Hierapolis, a town in the neighbourhood of Ephesus, from whence the Gospel of St. John was sent forth ; and the earliest record we have about the martyrdom of Papias sets it down about the same time as that of Polycarp, *i.e.*, about A.D. 160.

Now, it is difficult to conceive a statement more utterly groundless and arbitrary than this, that the silence of Papias as to the Gospel of St. John is a proof against its genuineness. For, in the first place, any notice of John's Gospel lay altogether out of the direction of Papias' researches ; and, secondly, we have no right to conclude, from Eusebius' extracts out of Papias' book, that there was no reference to St. John's Gospel in the entire book. The notices of St. Matthew and St. Mark which Eusebius quotes from Papias are not introduced to prove their authenticity, but only for the particular details which he mentions. It is quite possible that this writing did not contain the same kind of reference to St. John's writings, and this is all that the silence of Eusebius proves. Let us only add that Eusebius, in his extracts from Papias, makes no reference to St. Luke's Gospel. Are we, therefore, to conclude that Papias knew nothing of this Gospel also? And yet we are logically bound to draw this conclusion, absurd as it is, in both cases.

We have only one point more to touch upon here. At the end of his notice of Papias, Eusebius remarks that this writer has made use of passages taken from the First Epistle of John and the First Epistle of Peter. Does not this fact bear against us who refuse to see any force in his silence as to St. Luke, St. Paul, and the Gospel of St. John? Quite the contrary. No one in the early Church era doubted these writings, and so it never occurred to Eusebius to collect testimonies in their favour. But it was otherwise with the Catholic Epistles, the Apocalypse, and the Epistle to the Hebrews ; and it was of importance to adduce testimonies in their favour. But it may be said this proceeding is arbitrary. No, we answer ; and in favour of the justice of our point of view we have two arguments to adduce. Eusebius only says one thing of Polycarp's letter to the Philippians—that it contains passages taken from the First Epistle of Peter ; and yet the letter is full of quotations from St. Paul ! He also mentions (iv. 26), that Theophilus, in his letter to his friend Autolycus, made use of the Apocalypse, and yet he does not so much as notice that these books contain a citation of a passage from the Gospel of St. John, and even with the name of the apostle given. Now, the blind zeal of the adversaries of the Gospel has either chosen not to see this, or has passed it over in silence.

But there is another argument which we can appeal to. Eusebius has told us that Papias made use of St. John's First Epistle. Now, there are strong reasons, as we have seen above, for concluding that the Gospel and the Epistle came from the same hand. The testimony, therefore, of Papias in favour of the Epistle really amounts to one in favour of the Gospel. It is quite possible that those critics who treat history so freely, after having set aside the greater number of St. Paul's Epistles, can also treat in the same way the Gospel of St. John, though unquestioned hitherto. They have done so ; but in the face of such prejudice, and a determination to see only from their own point of view, we have nothing more to say.

CHAPTER V

Such, then, are the weapons which we employ against
an unbelieving criticism. But to complete our plan,
and maintain the truth of the Gospel, we must procure a new weapon, or, rather, open a new arsenal
of defence. It bears the name of New Testament
Textual Criticism. It is not easy to make this at
once clear to all readers : we must endeavour to do so.

The name denotes that branch of learning which is
concerned.with the originals of the sacred text. The
inquiry into these originals should teach us what the
Christian Church in various times and in different
lands has found written in those books which contain
the New Testament. Thus, for instance, it should
teach us what was the text used by Columba in the
sixth century, by Ambrose and Augustine in the
fourth, and by Cyprian and Tertullian, in their Latin
copies, in the third and second century ; or what
the Patriarch Photius in the tenth, Cyril, Bishop of
Jerusalem, in the fifth, Athanasius in the fourth, and
Origen in the third, had before them in the Greek
text. The chief end of such inquiries, however, lies
in its enabling us to find out the very words and expressions which the holy apostles either wrote or
dictated to their amanuenses. If the New Testament
is the most sacred and precious book in the world,
we should surely desire to possess the original text
of each of its books, in the state in which it left its
author's hands, without either addition or blank, or
change of any kind. I have already spoken of this

in the account of my travel and researches, to which I here refer the reader.

If you ask me, then, whether any popular version, such as Luther's, does or does not contain the original text, my answer is, Yes and No. I say Yes, as far as concerns your soul's salvation ; all that is needful for that, you have in Luther's version. But I also say No, for this reason, that Luther made his translation from a text which needed correction in many places. For this Greek text which Luther used was no better than the received text of the sixteenth century, based on the few manuscripts then accessible. We have already told you that this text differs in many places from the oldest authorities of the fourth, fifth, and sixth centuries, and, therefore, must be replaced by a text which is really drawn from the oldest sources discoverable. The difficulty of finding such a text lies in this, that there is a great diversity among these texts ; we have, therefore, to compare them closely together, and decide on certain points of superiority on which to prefer one text to another.

We have in this, then, a fixed point of the greatest importance, on which we can safely take our stand, that the Latin text, called the old Italic version, as found in a certain class of manuscripts, was already in use as early as the second century. The text of the old Italic is substantially that which Tertullian, about the end of the second century, and the Latin translator of Irenæus still earlier, made use of. If we had any Greek text of the second century to compare with this old Italic version, we should then be able to arrive at the original Greek text at that time in use. We should thus be able to approach very nearly to the original text which came from the apostle's hands, since it is certain that the text of the second century must resemble more closely that of the first than any later text can be expected to do. Such a manuscript is before us in the Sinaitic copy, which more than any other is in close agreement with the old Italic version. We do not mean that there are no other versions which agree as closely with the Sinaitic copy as the old Italic version, which the translator, who lived in North Africa, somewhere near our modern city of Algiers, had before him. For we find that the old Syriac version which has been recently found is quite as closely related as the Italic. The fathers of the Egyptian Church of the second and third century, moreover, establish the trustworthiness of this Sinaitic text.

What, then, do these considerations lead us to? In the first place they establish this—that as early as the middle of the second century our four Gospels existed in a Syriac and in a Latin version. This fact proves, not only what the harmonists of the latter half of the second century also prove, that our Gospels had already been received into the Canon, but they also decide that point which has been raised as to the genuineness of our present copies of St. Matthew and St. Mark's Gospels. We have seen how certain critics, on the authority of certain loose expressions of Papias, have said that our present Gospels are only versions of the original documents. Against this supposition these two versions enter an emphatic protest. At least at the time when these versions were produced, our present Gospels of Matthew and Mark must have been considered genuine. This being settled, it is a groundless and unreasonable supposition that, about the beginning of the second century, there were two entirely different copies of St. Matthew and St. Mark in existence : for then we should have to admit that these authentic copies disappeared, leaving not a trace behind, while other spurious copies took their place, and were received everywhere instead of the genuine originals.

We have only one more inference to draw from the state of the text of these early documents, the old Greek, Syriac, and Latin copies. Although these set forth the text which was in general use about the middle of the second century, we may well suppose that before this text came into use it had a history of its own. I mean that the text passed from one hand to another, and was copied again and again, and so must have suffered from all these revisions. I can only here assert this as the result of my long experience in dealing with manuscripts, without going into details to prove that it was so. But I must here make the assertion as one of the most important results of my critical labours. If no one before me has been able to establish this point in the same way, this is owing to my fortunate discovery of the Sinaitic copy. Now, if my assertion on this point has any solid base to rest upon, we may confidently say, that by the end of the first century our four Gospels were in use in the Church. I here advance nothing new. For confirmation of what I say, I refer my reader to what I have already advanced, and endeavoured to make clear and apparent to all.

And now I draw my argument to a close. Should it fall into the hands of learned opponents, they will doubtless say that I have left out much that is important. This seems to me to be mere trifling. It has been easy for writers with a little subtlety and apparent seriousness to set forth the alleged contradictions and mistakes in early Church history, but which are in truth their own. In this they have used all sorts of devices, and easily succeeded in deceiving the ignorant. And it is to meet these special pleadings that historical testimony becomes so important.

A single well-established fact weighs more in the scale of good sense than the most dazzling wit, or the most ingenious sophistry, with which they torture and twist the facts which occurred eighteen hundred years ago.

May my writing serve this end, to make you mistrust those novel theories upon, or rather against, the Gospels, which would persuade you that the wonderful details which the Gospels give us of our gracious Saviour are founded on ignorance or deceit. The Gospels, like the Only-Begotten of the Father, will endure as long as human nature itself, while the discoveries of this pretended wisdom must sooner or later disappear like bubbles. He who has made shipwreck of his own faith, and who lives only after the flesh, cannot endure to see others trusting in their Saviour. Do not, then, let yourself be disturbed by their clamour, but rather hold what you have, the more firmly because others assail it. Do not think that we are dubious about the final victory of truth. For this result there is One pledged to whom the whole world is mere feebleness. All that concerns our duty is, to bear testimony to the truth, to the best of our ability, and that not for victory, but for conscience' sake.

THE MOUNT SINAI MANUSCRIPT
OF THE BIBLE

❡ *The Discovery*

THE fortunes and migrations of any important ancient manuscript must always offer matter of romantic interest, but the circumstances attending the discovery of the Codex Sinaiticus have given it a popular appeal surpassing that of either of its sisters, the Codex Vaticanus and the Codex Alexandrinus. Were it possible to accept the tradition which represents the latter as written by the martyr Thecla shortly after the Council of Nicaea (A.D. 325), that manuscript would indeed possess a unique interest; but it seems out of the question to entertain for it an earlier date than at best the beginning of the fifth century. Whereas the Vaticanus has remained (save for a period during the Napoleonic wars) in the security of the Vatican Library since the fifteenth century, and the Alexandrinus, ever since it was presented in 1627 to Charles I of England by Cyril Lucar, Patriarch successively of Alexandria and Constantinople, has formed part first of the Royal Library and subsequently of that of the British Museum, the Sinai manuscript was not discovered till the year 1844. It is indeed likely, though not certain, that it had been seen nearly a century before by the Italian traveller, Vitaliano Donati, but it remained totally unknown to the world at large until, in May 1844, the great German Biblical scholar, Constantine Tischendorf, during a visit to the monastery of St Catherine on Mount Sinai, found 129 leaves of it in a waste-paper basket, about to be consigned to the furnace, in which two other basketfuls (so the librarian told him) had already been consumed. Forty-three of these leaves he obtained as a gift and afterwards presented them to the King of Saxony; but he was unable, either then or on a subsequent visit in 1853, to obtain possession of the others or to discover whether anything further remained of the manuscript from which they were taken. In 1859, however, he revisited the monastery with a letter of introduction from the Tsar; and on the evening of 4 February

3

he was shown the whole volume, so far as it then survived, that is, the 86 leaves which he had been unable to bring away with him, and 261 other leaves, making in all 347. Thus it has come about that a small portion of the manuscript is preserved in the University Library at Leipzig, where it is known as the Codex Friderico-Augustanus, whereas the remainder has hitherto been in the former Imperial Library at Leningrad, save for one fragment, now in the Library of the Society of Ancient Literature in that city.

¶ *The Acquisition by the Russian Government*
The slanders which have been widely uttered against a distinguished scholar and honourable man make it necessary to describe somewhat in detail the subsequent history of the manuscript, down to the time when it finally became the property of the Tsar of Russia.

Any moral claim that the monastery had to complain of the loss of so historical a treasure is obviously destroyed by the fact that the monks had thrown away a great part of it. But it was actually alleged by Tischendorf's enemies that on the occasion of his visit in 1859 he stole the manuscript. There is no vestige of truth in the allegation. His account of the affair (and there is no other contemporary record) may be read in his own words in his book on the manuscript.[1] That his account is true, no one can doubt who reads it with an impartial mind; for he attempts to conceal nothing. He admits that he tried to buy the Codex from the monastery and the steward. When both these refused, he asked leave to bring it away to Cairo. Dionysius, the Superior of the monastery, was absent at Cairo; all present agreed to his request except Vitalius, the monk in charge of the church furniture, in whose special library the manuscript had been preserved. Owing to this opposition, Tischendorf was unable to bring it away with him to Cairo, whither he accordingly went to obtain permission from the Superior. This was readily given; the Superior dispatched a camel-messenger, and on 24 February 1859 the manuscript was placed in Tischendorf's hands for copying. But it was long before he was able to bring it away from Cairo. It was agreed at a meeting at the

[1] *Die Sinaibibel*, Leipzig, 1871, pp. 14 ff. See also the introduction to his *Notitia Editionis Codicis Bibliorum Sinaitici*, Leipzig, 1860.

PORTRAIT OF TISCHENDORF AS A YOUNG MAN
By kind permission of DR. LUDWIG SCHNELLER

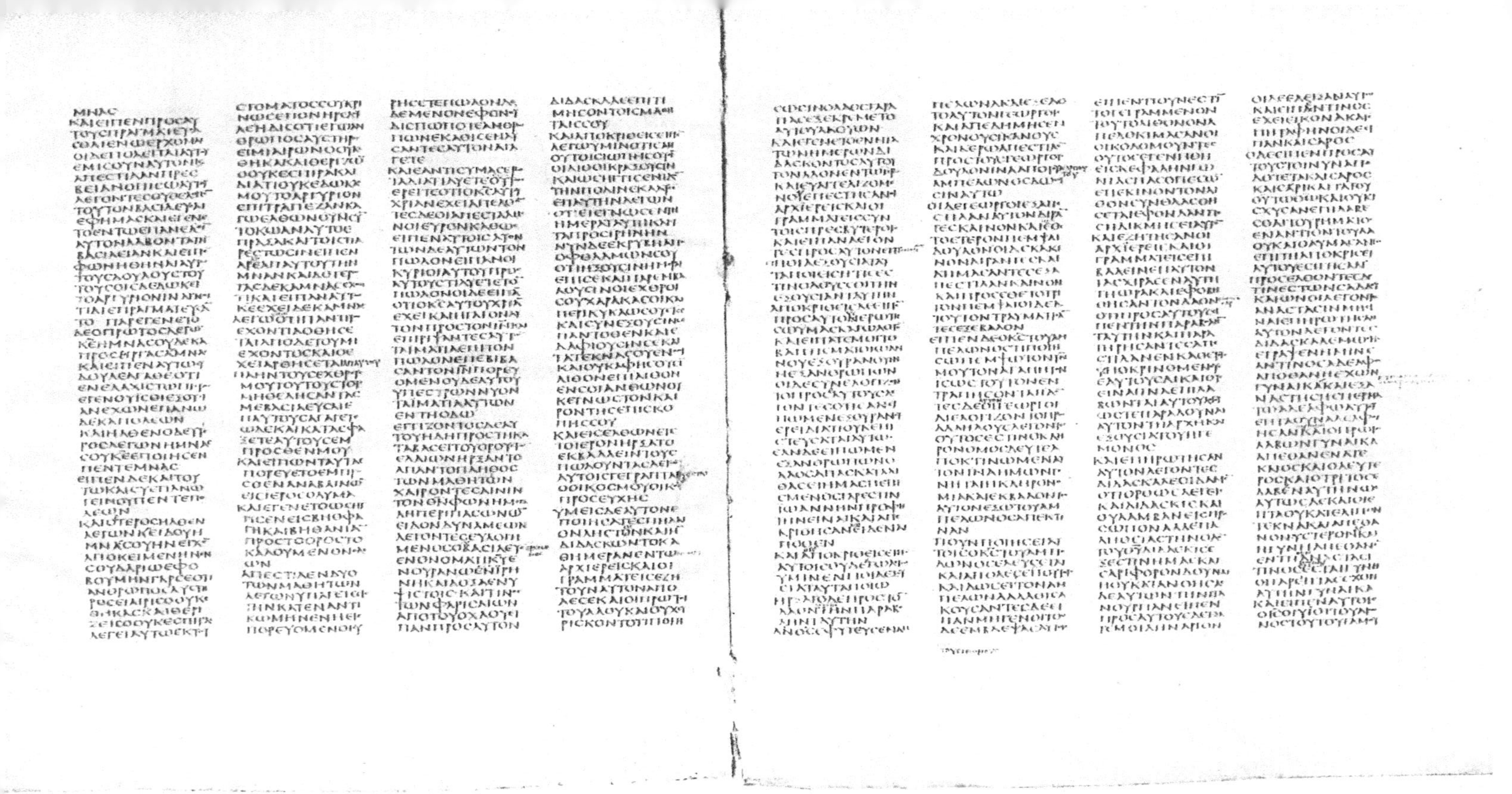

CODEX SINAITICUS. LUKE XIX. 13—XX. 34

Russian Consulate that he should be allowed to have single gatherings of eight leaves at a time to copy. It is worth mentioning that while this was going on, a young English scholar got sight of the manuscript and tried to buy it. The Prior assured Tischendorf that the brethren would rather make a present of it to the Tsar than sell it for English gold. The tradition in the Tischendorf family is that the disappointed scholar joined the ranks of the German savant's enemies.[1]

The proposal to present the Codex to the Tsar, which Tischendorf had already broached to the brethren before this incident, could not be carried out at the time, because the old Abbot (who also had the title of Archbishop) of Sinai, Constantius, had died at Constantinople, and only a fully consecrated Archbishop could sanction such a transaction. The monks chose one Cyril as his successor, but their choice had to be confirmed by the Sublime Porte, and it was bitterly opposed by the Patriarch of Jerusalem, who according to traditional use had the duty of consecrating the Archbishop of Sinai. The monks gave Tischendorf to understand that the donation of the manuscript to the Tsar would be seriously considered after the election of the new Archbishop had been confirmed. They thought that the matter might be settled in three months. Tischendorf went off to Palestine, Smyrna, and Patmos. It was during this time (in May) that he was seen by Mr. James Finn, Consul for Jerusalem and Palestine, at Jerusalem.[2] Mr. Finn's diary contains a somewhat confused account of the case.

[1] Various correspondents have pointed out that in 1847 there was some talk of George Borrow being sent on a mission to the East in quest of manuscripts for the British Museum, and one of the places he was to visit was the monastery on Mount Sinai. The proposal came to nothing; but had he gone, much trouble and expense might have been saved, and we should have had an interesting account of his experiences. (W. I. Knapp, *Life . . . of George Borrow*, 1899, vol. ii, pp. 61–3.)

[2] Diary of Mr. Finn, quoted by Miss Constance Finn in *The Times*, 1 February 1934. Her letter is inaccurate in giving the impression that he had the Codex with him; what the diary actually says is that Tischendorf had had the Codex 'conveyed to St Petersburgh in original'. Even this is incorrect; as we shall see, Tischendorf did not take the Codex until September of that year. A year later, 1 May 1860, the Archimandrite Porphyrius Uspenski (afterwards Bishop of Chirgin) told the diarist that he had discovered the Codex some time before and published something about it. This is the usual claim put forward in such circumstances by some one who 'knew about it all the time'. Doubtless after Tischendorf found the 129 leaves in the waste-paper basket in 1844,

On his return to Cairo at the end of July, Tischendorf learned that the question of the vacant see was no farther advanced, and was begged by the Archbishop-elect himself to forward his interests. He not unwillingly went to Constantinople and placed the two intimately connected objects of his visit, the confirmation of the Archbishop and the proposed transfer of the Codex, in the hands of Prince Lobanow, the Russian Ambassador. The Patriarch, however, stood firm, and there seemed to remain no solution except one suggested by Tischendorf, to wit, the summoning of the Holy Synod and a personal appeal to it by the Archbishop. This meant a further delay of months, which Tischendorf could not contemplate with equanimity. He therefore obtained from the Russian Ambassador an official letter, dated 10/22 September, to the monks of Mount Sinai, asking them to lend the Codex, which they were proposing to offer to the Tsar, to Tischendorf, that he might take it to St. Petersburg to control the printing of it, and undertaking that the Codex should remain the property of the brotherhood of Mount Sinai until the Superior should offer it officially in the name of the brotherhood to the Tsar. If unforeseen circumstances should hinder the fulfilment of this intention, the Codex should be without fail restored to the brethren.

Tischendorf's efforts on behalf of the brethren had been favourably reported to them by their representatives at Constantinople; and on 28 September the Codex was handed to him. Cyril, accepting the plan suggested by Tischendorf, left immediately for Constantinople, and two months later the Holy Synod, with the Patriarch as sole dissentient, confirmed his election. In December the Archbishop wrote to Tischendorf 'La sainte cause a triomphé'. But the other part of the bargain remained unfulfilled, and nothing was done about the donation of the Codex.

Porphyrius or others looked for the rest and found it. What Porphyrius did do was, after Tischendorf's first visit, to find in the binding of another book fragments of two leaves. This was in 1845. In 1863 he published a Russian brochure attacking the orthodoxy of the Codex. Porphyrius also told Mr. Finn that Tischendorf arrived at Sinai just when the Archbishopric was vacant, and promised Cyril, the ambitious president of the convent, to have him made Archbishop if he would make a present of the manuscript to the Russian Emperor. 'This bargain has been fulfilled on both sides.' We have to thank Miss Finn for permission to consult the actual text of the diary.

On 19 November Tischendorf handed it to the Tsar. But it is significant of the correct attitude maintained throughout by the Imperial Government, that it was regarded as property entrusted to it, and therefore was not placed in the Imperial Library, but deposited in a fireproof vault in the Ministry of Foreign Affairs, where it remained until the donation was finally made.

It has been remarked by Professor C. R. Gregory[1] that 'in the East a gift demands a return, and that this return may under given circumstances be extraordinarily like a good round price paid for the nominal gift'. This being so, and the negotiations being conducted between the Russian Foreign Office on the one hand, and Oriental monks on the other, it is not surprising that they lasted a long time. Probably the monks complained of pressure being brought to bear on them; that they even went so far as to refuse indignantly the sum which was offered to them, and demand the return of the Codex, can be true only in so far as such gestures are part of the ordinary conduct of a bargain in Oriental countries.

Meanwhile, the Monastery of St Catherine was not a happy community. The Archbishop Cyril only held the see from 1860–1867,[2] when he was deposed, and succeeded by Callistratus, though Cyril continued to call himself Archbishop. The new Archbishop was a firm friend of Tischendorf, as may be gathered from his letter of 15 July 1869:[3]

'We hasten to assure you that We and Our reverend brethren cherish for ever thankful memories of you, that We consider Ourselves fortunate to have found such a friend and patron. . . . That your dear and learned Excellence is our good friend and honoured champion is manifest again from what is related to Us in your valued letter concerning the first edition of the precious Bible and your exertions on behalf of Sinai with His Majesty the Emperor of all the Russias, to whom finally, as you know, this famous Bible has been presented as a testimony of the eternal gratitude of Ourselves and Sinai. The results of these exertions have been duly communicated to Us also, but nothing has yet been despatched, neither the decoration nor the Imperial

[1] *Canon and Text of the New Testament*, Edinburgh, 1907, p. 331.
[2] P. Gregoriades, Ἡ ἱερὰ Μονὴ τοῦ Σινᾶ, Jerusalem, 1875, pp. 148–9.
[3] Tischendorf, op. cit., p. 91; C. R. Gregory, in his edition of Tischendorf's *New Testament*, vol. iii, pt. 1, Leipzig 1884, p. 352. Tischendorf gives the translation of part of the letter, Gregory the original Greek of a part, the two supplementing each other.

gift. In so far we consider Ourselves fortunate, in enjoying the sublime and powerful Imperial favour, of which we have so great need, for the Holy Monastery of Sinai.'

So they had not yet received their reward; but Tischendorf was working for them. On 5/17 December 1869 Count Ignatiew wrote to him from Pera[1] acknowledging a letter of 13 November in which Tischendorf had regretted that the compensation accorded by the Tsar to the Archbishop of Sinai for the acquisition of the manuscript was so long delayed. Ignatiew, sharing his regret, explained that for some years the monastery had been in a state of complete and scandalous anarchy, ending in the deposition of Archbishop Cyril and the election of the present titular, Callistratus; but Cyril claimed that his deposition was uncanonical, and continued to call himself Archbishop of Mount Sinai. It was but recently that Callistratus had been recognized by the Sublime Porte and the Egyptian Government. In such circumstances, it had been impossible to wind up the affair; 'to whom were we to send the money and the decorations?' Ignatiew demanded a formal document by which the whole community should declare that it made a gift of the manuscript to Russia. All he had received so far was one in which the signature of the monks of St Catherine was wanting. But the Archbishop, when Ignatiew on his last visit to Cairo pointed this out, had sent an express messenger to Mount Sinai; no doubt by now all was arranged, and the money and decorations, which had been left with the Russian Consul General, with full instructions, had been delivered to the Archbishop. The money amounted, he adds, to 9,000 roubles, 7,000 for the library of the principal monastery, and 2,000 for the dependency of Mount Thabor. The Archbishop and the members of the community of Djouvania whom he had seen, showed themselves completely satisfied with this gift, and expressed their gratitude to him in the warmest terms.

The sum of money is estimated by Professor Gregory[2] as equivalent to $6,750 or more than £1,350 sterling, 'for that time a high price

---

[1] We have to thank the Librarian of Leipzig University, Dr. Glauning, for photostats of the four letters (three originals and one copy) to Tischendorf, which are quoted in what follows.   [2] Op. cit., p. 332.

to pay for the manuscript. . . . The decorations referred to above are valued in the East even more highly than they are in the decoration-loving circles of Western Europe, and the monks received a number of these decorations.'

The formal deed of gift[1] was signed on 18 November 1869 by the monks of Mount Sinai, who acknowledged to have presented (*fait hommage*) to His Majesty the Emperor of Russia a manuscript of the Old and New Testaments discovered by Professor Tischendorf, in return for which donation His Majesty the Emperor granted to the Library of Mount Sinai the sum of 7,000 roubles and to the Convent of Mount Thabor 2,000 roubles. The Imperial Government held a receipt for the said amounts. In addition to this pecuniary recompense some of the Sinaite Fathers obtained Russian decorations.

And there can be no doubt that the transaction had closed to the complete satisfaction of the monks, or at any rate of the Archbishop Callistratus. For Tischendorf remained on the friendliest terms with him. In the Leipzig University Library are three letters from the Archbishop, of 14 October 1870, of December 1870, and of 12 March 1874.

The first, in Greek, with many flattering expressions of gratitude to Tischendorf and the Russian Vice-Consul, informs him that the Archbishop is going to Mount Sinai to keep the feast of St Catherine, asks that the expression of the gratitude of himself and all the brethren may be communicated to the proper quarters, and says that the writer and all his holy brotherhood will never cease to pray for the Majesty of the Emperor of all the Russias, who has in the East such servants as these who so warmly champion the cause of the holy tabernacles of the Orthodox Faith, and so worthily represent His Majesty. The second, also in Greek, is equally friendly to Tischendorf, and tells a long story of quarrels with the Patriarch of Alexandria, for protection against whom the Archbishop was appealing to Ignatiew (thus showing that he bore no grudge against him for the Codex agreement). He adds that if Tischendorf could persuade the

---

[1] See the note communicated 1/13 June 1878 by the Russian Ministry of Foreign Affairs to Professor Gregory, and printed in his edition of Tischendorf's *New Testament*, loc. cit., pp. 351–2.

Tsar to send them some pecuniary assistance, they would regard him (Tischendorf) as their greatest benefactor. The third, in French, in similar flattering terms, thanks him for his friendly exertions with the Ambassador Ignatiew. 'Notre affaire reste encore presque dans le même point, et à cause de cet état passif, où nous nous trouvons, nous ne savons pas ce qui nous arriverait dans l'autre jour.' But they hope that Tischendorf's friendly intervention with His Excellency will have a good effect.

The affair to which the Archbishop alludes was probably the quarrel with the Patriarch of Alexandria mentioned in the previous letter; it cannot have been connected with the Codex, the donation of which had been long ago settled. In any case, as Dr. Glauning observes, the continuance of such relations between Tischendorf and the Archbishop as these letters reveal is only conceivable on the presupposition that the community of Sinai did not feel that it had been cheated or over-reached by Tischendorf, and this presupposition includes the further one, that the affair of the transfer of ownership of the Codex Sinaiticus had also been brought by St Petersburg to a settlement free from all objection or dissatisfaction.

Finally, to bring the story down to recent times, we may quote the evidence of a visitor to the monastery as late as 1926.[1]

'I have a distinct recollection of the conversation one day turning to the question of the MSS. in the renowned library, and the story of Dr. Tischendorf and his epoch-making discovery of the Codex and its subsequent presentation, in return for a Royal donation, to the Tsar, was naturally recounted. The fact that the current story of the transaction was similar to the one then accepted by the monks of Mount Sinai themselves renders it all the more surprising, if not inconsistent, that his Beatitude, as head of the same community, should bring forward, so belatedly, this claim to the ownership of what his predecessors had apparently disposed of, in a manner and at an evaluation, which they then considered to be completely satisfactory.'

It is surely obvious that the question of transfer of ownership which was settled by deed of gift more than sixty years ago cannot reasonably be reopened at the present time, even if there were no such thing as a Statute of Limitations. This is the attitude which we are bound to assume to the charges which have been made, to the effect

[1] Mr. John Walker, in *The Times* for 31 Jan. 1934.

MONASTERY OF ST. CATHERINE ON MOUNT SINAI

Reproduction of a lithograph from a picture by A. DAUZATS,
exhibited at the Paris Salon in 1845

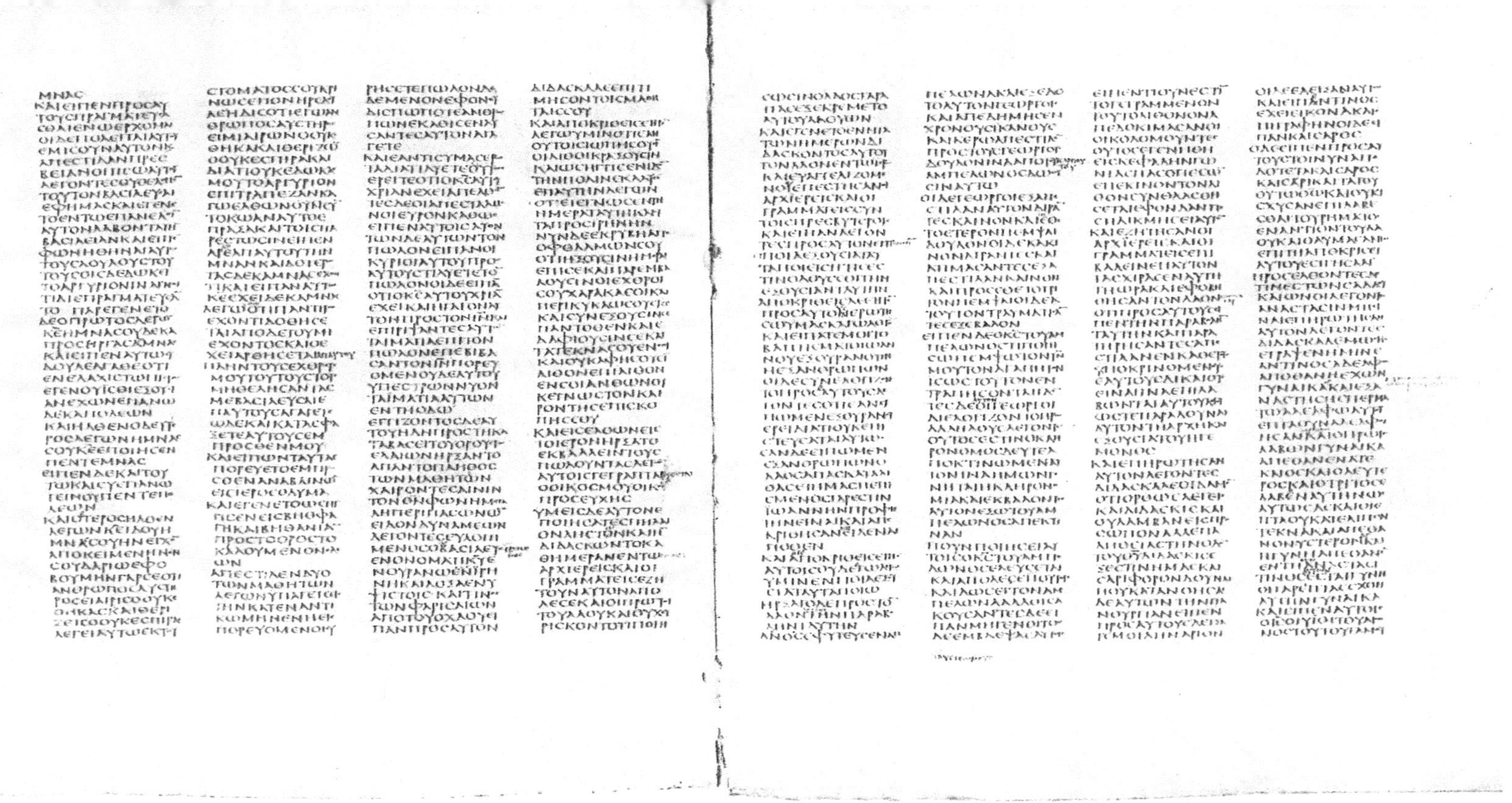

CODEX SINAITICUS. LUKE XIX. 13—XX. 34

that the gift was extorted by the Russian Government, on pain of confiscation of property belonging to the monastery; and also to the alleged admission by Count Ignatiew, in private letters to the Archimandrite Antoninos, that he had 'stolen' the Codex—a statement which it is difficult to believe that one of the astutest diplomats of the nineteenth century would have made in all seriousness, even to a bosom friend. The publication of these letters seems to have provoked no action on the part of the Monastery at the time (1909), and, in any case, the complete and cordial acceptance of the position by the Archbishop of Sinai in the letters quoted above renders such allegations beside the point at issue.

¶ The Genuineness of the Manuscript

Apart from a recent newspaper report that it is a copy made by a forger in a Bolshevik prison from an earlier copy of the fifteenth or sixteenth century, a story sufficiently refuted by the appearance of the leaves themselves and a comparison of them with the Oxford facsimile of the Codex Sinaiticus, which was prepared before the War, the suspicion which has been aroused as to the genuineness of the manuscript rests solely on the declaration of Constantine Simonides in the middle of the nineteenth century that he had himself written it. His claim was sufficiently refuted at the time by competent scholars; nor, though the science of palaeography has since then advanced greatly and the manuscript has been minutely studied, had any doubt as to its authenticity been subsequently expressed till the fantastic story of Simonides was revived by a section of the Press. The story in its complete form (details were added to meet objections from time to time both by Simonides himself and by a monk Callinicus, who appears to have been a sort of 'Mrs. Harris', i.e. Simonides himself under a different name) was that about the end of 1839 his uncle Benedict, head of the monastery of Panteleëmon on Mount Athos, wishing to give a present to the Tsar Nicholas I, decided on 'a copy of the Old and New Testaments, written according to the ancient form, in capital letters, and on parchment', together with the remains of the seven Apostolic Fathers. Dionysius, the calligrapher of the monastery, declined the task as too difficult, whereupon Simonides, then studying theology under his uncle, agreed to undertake it. He mastered the art of calligraphy, found in the library of the monastery a large volume of vellum, which had for the most part been conveniently left blank, and proceeded to copy out the Old and New Testaments, using as his model 'a copy of the Moscow edition of both Testaments (published and presented to the Greeks by the illustrious brothers Zosimas)', which his uncle had collated 'with the ancient ones' [editions or manuscripts?]. To the Biblical scriptures he added the Epistle of Barnabas and the first part of the 'Shepherd' of Hermas, but then ran short of vellum and therefore did not proceed with the other Apostolic Fathers. His uncle, who corrected the manuscript in many places, died 29 August 1840; and some time afterwards Simonides went to Constantinople, where he showed the manuscript to the Patriarchs Anthimus and Constantius. The latter, who had been 'Bishop [really Archbishop] of Sinai', urged that it should be presented to St Catherine's monastery. This Simonides agreed to do, and after an unspecified interval he delivered the manuscript to the Patriarch, who acknowledged it in a letter dated 13 August 1841. On a subsequent visit in 1846 Simonides learned that the Patriarch 'had sent [the manuscript] some time previously to Mount Sinai'. There, in 1852, Simonides, while on a visit, saw it himself and 'found it much altered, having an older appearance than it ought to have. The dedication to the Emperor Nicholas, placed at the beginning of the book, had been removed'.

This ingenious fable teems with improbabilities. In the year 1839–40 Simonides, born 11 November 1824,[1] was fifteen years old. He arrived at Mount Athos, according to a biography by Charles Stewart, circulated by himself, in November 1839 and studied theology under Benedict. Benedict, so Simonides assured the world,

[1] In a letter published in *The Literary Churchman*, 2 February 1863, pp. 48–51, Simonides replies to arguments adduced against his claim and *inter alia* declares that the true date of his birth was 5 November 1820. But he had himself previously (*Athenaeum*, 21 December 1861, p. 849) given the date as 11 November 1824. The later letter contradicts his own earlier narrative in several particulars; e.g. in the latter he says 'I began to practise the principles of caligraphy', whereas in his subsequent letter he claims to have been already a skilled calligrapher. His attempts to explain this and other discrepancies are lame in the extreme.

12

discovered many ancient manuscripts, which, on the failure of his eyes, he set his nephew to reading and copying; yet simultaneously, that is, between the end of 1839, when the present to the Tsar was resolved on, and 29 August 1840, when Benedict died, Simonides found time to learn the art of calligraphy and to copy the whole of the Old and New Testaments in time for many corrections to be introduced by his uncle before his death. And this at the age of little more than fifteen!

Furthermore, Simonides, when he states that he saw again in 1852 the manuscript which he had himself written twelve years before, clearly implies that it was at that time complete save for the dedication; yet Tischendorf had in 1844 taken away forty-three leaves of it, which he found, with many others, in a waste-paper basket. 'Callinicus', in a letter written after Simonides had published his first story (*The Literary Churchman*, 16 January 1863, p. 23), declared that Tischendorf stole these leaves; and Simonides himself, in another letter (ibid., 2 February 1863, p. 47), writes: 'I saw [the manuscript] in safe preservation when I was at the monastery in March, 1844, a little before Tischendorf's arrival.' Yet in his first story we are told that in 1846 he learned from Constantius of the dispatch of the manuscript to Sinai. The inference is obvious that when he wrote his original narrative he did not know of Tischendorf's first find of the leaves, and that he subsequently invented his own visit in 1844 and the testimony of Callinicus in order to bridge this gap in his first story. Moreover, in 1845 Porphyrius Uspenski found in the monastery fragments of two leaves of the manuscript, both from the Pentateuch, used in the bindings of other books and showing every sign of having been there for a considerable time; and in 1859 more than half the Old Testament was missing. How had this happened to a manuscript written in 1840 and seen by Simonides himself in 1852, still more or less intact? And how comes it that on many pages of a manuscript so recent the ink has faded to so marked an extent?

There are, however, other difficulties. The alleged Moscow edition which Simonides claimed to have used as his model has never been identified. No book, printed or manuscript, is known from which the text of the Codex Sinaiticus could conceivably have been derived, and some of its readings are in fact unique. All palaeographers who have studied the manuscript are agreed that at least three different hands can be distinguished in the main text. Why did the handwriting of Simonides himself change in this way? And how are we to explain the fact that the numerous corrections are in hands of various types, from the fourth century till well into the Middle Ages?

It may be added that a monk Callinicus who was eventually found in St Catherine's monastery declared that he had not written the letters so signed and did not know Simonides; that the brethren all agreed that no such person as Simonides had ever visited Sinai; that the manuscript was entered in ancient catalogues of the monastic library; and further that S. Nicolaides, formerly Archdeacon and first Secretary of the Metropolis of Salonica, who had five times visited Mount Athos and was well acquainted with all the monasteries, ridiculed Simonides' story and threw doubts on the very existence of Benedict (*The Parthenon*, 28 February 1863).

Such points as have been stated above can be appreciated by all, whether skilled in palaeography or not; the palaeographical arguments against Simonides' claim, which only experts can fully assess, are even more decisive, and it may be categorically stated that no single person qualified to judge feels any doubt whatever as to the genuineness of the manuscript. One point of detail may, however, be alluded to, as it constitutes a palaeographical test which is in itself fatal to Simonides' story. One of the arguments used in favour of the theory that the manuscript was written in Egypt is the sporadic occurrence in it, both in the text itself and in the earlier corrections, of an omega of very curious shape (ѡ as against the usual ω). This very rare form is found in one or two papyri from Egypt, notably in Papyrus 28 of the John Rylands Library, Manchester, but, apart from a few instances in the Codex Vaticanus, it appears to be unknown elsewhere. Now in 1839–40, the Codex Vaticanus was locked away and inaccessible to scholars in the Vatican Library, and the papyri in question were buried in the sands of Egypt. Whence then could Simonides have obtained it? Or what object could he have in inventing so strange a form?

Apart from the ridiculous story of the forger in the Bolshevik prison, the suspicion attaching to the Codex rests wholly on the rambling and sometimes self-contradictory assertions of a man convicted of gross lying and forgery, which have been rejected with contempt by every expert who has studied the original manuscript. In fact, as Professor Kirsopp Lake has written, 'the details of this absurd story belong rather to the annals of crime than to the history of palaeography'.

¶ *Description of the Manuscript*

The whole volume as it now exists, including the leaves at Leipzig, that belonging to the Society of Ancient Literature, and two fragmentary leaves found in the bindings of other manuscripts, contains 393 leaves, of which 347 have been acquired by the British Museum from the Russian Government through Messrs. Maggs Brothers.

Before Tischendorf's visit to Sinai a good deal of the manuscript had already disappeared. What is left includes the whole of the New Testament, with two works which very nearly obtained admission into the Canon, the Epistle of Barnabas and the 'Shepherd' of Hermas, the latter incomplete. Of the Old Testament the following books remain, in the order here given: Genesis (fragment), Numbers (fragment), 1 Chronicles (portions), Ezra (ix. 9–end), Nehemiah, Esther, Tobit, Judith, 1 and 4 Maccabees, Isaiah, Jeremiah, Lamentations (portions), the Minor Prophets (except Hosea, Amos, and Micah), Psalms, Proverbs, Ecclesiastes, Song of Songs, Wisdom, Ecclesiasticus, Job. Of these, the leaves at Leipzig contain the whole of Nehemiah and Esther and portions of Chronicles, Ezra, Tobit, Jeremiah, and Lamentations.

The leaves are composed of very fine vellum, varying in thickness but usually thin and each measuring 15 by 13½ inches, made up for the most part in gatherings or quires of eight leaves or sixteen pages. The text is written (except in the seven books, Psalms–Job, where there are only two columns) in four narrow columns to the page, so that a complete opening shows eight successive columns;

15

and each column normally contains 48 lines. At least three different scribes, writing very similar hands and employing an ink of the brownish tint characteristic of the period, were employed on the main text, besides others responsible for such minutiae as the running titles, section numbers, and subscriptions, not to mention numerous correctors, contemporary and later. The script is a rather large and handsome uncial, regular and exact but a little heavy. It represents a type of hand found in Greek papyri written in Egypt at least as far back as the latter part of the second century; and were handwriting the only criterion of date, one might venture to put back the preparation of the volume to the end of the third century. This is, however, rendered impossible by the presence, apparently as an original part of the manuscript and certainly before it left the scriptorium, of the Eusebian apparatus, which consists of section numbers and references to the canons or tables devised by Eusebius of Caesarea for his harmony of the Gospels. The tables themselves are missing, perhaps through the early loss of a quire between the Old and New Testaments, but the section and reference numbers, which, like the titles of the Psalms, are in red ink, appear throughout the Gospels. The date at which Eusebius devised his scheme is unknown, but since he died about A.D. 340 and we must allow some time for his system to establish itself, we cannot well place the Sinai manuscript appreciably before that date.

It has generally been stated that the Codex Vaticanus is earlier than the Sinai manuscript, but this statement seems to rest mainly on the assumption, which we now know to be untrue, that the style of hand represented by the latter was of fourth-century origin, whereas the hand of the Vaticanus is of a rounder and less heavy type, which was believed to be earlier. The fact that the Vaticanus has a peculiar system of numbering in place of the Eusebian sections is of little moment at this early date. There seems in truth little ground for separating the two manuscripts by any great interval of time, and none for dogmatism. It is even possible that both were written in the same scriptorium, which there are various reasons, not conclusive but of some weight, for placing in Egypt, and, if so, presumably at Alexandria. At a later period, which considerations

16

of script fix as between the fifth and seventh centuries, the Codex Sinaiticus was very likely at Caesarea in Palestine, when corrections were made in it by various hands. This is inferred from two notes added by one (or two) of these correctors at the end of Ezra and Esther respectively. The second and longer may be rendered into English as follows: 'Collated with an exceedingly ancient copy which was corrected by the hand of the holy martyr Pamphilus; and at the end of the same ancient book, which began with the first book of Kings and ended with Esther, there is some such subscription as this, in the hand of the same martyr: *Taken and corrected from the Hexapla of Origen corrected by himself. Antoninus the Confessor collated it; I, Pamphilus, corrected the volume in prison through the great favour and enlargement of God; and if it may be said without offence it is not easy to find a copy comparable to this copy.* The same ancient copy differed from the present volume in respect of certain proper names'.

The Hexapla, the chief treasure of the great library at Caesarea, was the copy of the Old Testament prepared by Origen (about A.D. 185–254). It was written in six parallel columns, of which the first two contained the Hebrew text, respectively in Hebrew and in Greek characters, and the others the Greek translations of Aquila, Symmachus, the Septuagint (revised by Origen himself), and Theodotion. The Antoninus mentioned in the note was martyred at Caesarea on 13 November A.D. 309, Pamphilus on 16 February following; and thus we see that a portion of the Old Testament text (Kings to Esther) in the Sinai manuscript was corrected from a manuscript written before 309 and revised about that year, by comparison with the Hexapla itself, in the prison to which the two scholars had been consigned during the Great Persecution. These corrections have therefore a very special value.

¶ The Value of the Manuscript for the Text

Textually the manuscript would in any case be of considerable interest by the mere fact of its early date; but the character of the text gives it a value of a special kind. It is indeed a little misleading

17

to speak thus of its 'character', as if this were uniform throughout. The textual value of a manuscript depends upon that of its source or sources. Now, in the fourth century complete copies of the Bible were still a novelty, the sacred scriptures having hitherto circulated, for the most part, either as single books or in collections of a few books; and thus the text of the Sinai manuscript was derived, ultimately at least and perhaps directly, not from a single archetype of uniform character but from many manuscripts, each containing small portions of the Bible. Thus, it is not surprising to find that whereas in the Psalms the Sinai manuscript (denoted ℵ or Aleph) and the Vaticanus (B) combine to show a text which has been called Lower Egyptian, while that of the Alexandrinus (A) belongs to a different family, in the Major Prophets Aleph and A are often found combining in opposition to B. In the New Testament, for which Aleph is complete and which probably stands first in interest for most readers of this pamphlet, B and Aleph are the leading representatives of the type of text called by Westcott and Hort 'Neutral' and by them regarded as representing, more than any other, the original form of the New Testament. Of the two, B (for which Westcott and Hort had a decided preference) is the purer representative of the family, but it seems clear that Aleph, though it not infrequently differs from B, is derived from a common ancestor. Moreover it alone of the three early codices is complete, for B has lost the Pastoral Epistles and Revelation, and A wants the greater part of Matthew. Recently, owing mainly to the researches of Canon Streeter and Professor Kirsopp Lake, a text which has been called 'Caesarean', and which possesses strong claims to consideration, has been identified; and some early papyri found in Egypt, notably the Chester Beatty papyrus of the four Gospels and Acts recently edited by Sir Frederic Kenyon, though not belonging strictly to any of the recognized families, show a text which in many respects approximates to the Caesarean type. This raises a doubt as to the correctness of some of Westcott and Hort's views and makes it necessary to investigate the whole question afresh.

It will perhaps be of interest to set down here translations of a few passages, selected from many such, in which Aleph offers readings of interest. These translations and the text of the Authorized Version are printed in parallel columns, and agreements of Aleph with B are marked by an asterisk.

Sinai MS. (Aleph)	*A. V.*
*Matt. i. 25. Till she brought forth a son.	Till she had brought forth her first-born son.
*Matt. v. 44. But I say unto you, Love your enemies, and pray for them which persecute you.	But I say unto you, Love your enemies, bless them that curse you, do good to them that hate you, and pray for them which despitefully use you, and persecute you.
Matt. xii. 46–8. His mother and his brethren stood without. And he answered and said unto him that told him, &c. [B has the shorter text as above, except for the insertion after 'stood without' of 'desiring to speak with him'.]	His mother and his brethren stood without, desiring to speak with him. Then one said unto him, Behold, thy mother and thy brethren stand without, desiring to speak with thee. But he answered and said unto him that told him, &c.
*Matt. xviii. 11. [Omitted.]	For the Son of man is come to save that which was lost.
Mark xvi. 8–20. The Gospel ends with *v.* 8, which, literally translated, reads thus: And going out they fled from the sepulchre; for trembling and amazement held them: and they said nothing to any man; for they were afraid. B agrees. A (Codex Alexandrinus) has *vv.* 9–20, as in the Authorized Version.	
*Luke x. 41–2. Martha, Martha, thou art careful and troubled about many things: But there is need of few things or one: for Mary chose the good part.	Martha, Martha, thou art careful and troubled about many things: But one thing is needful: and Mary hath chosen that good part.
Luke xi. 2–4. Father, hallowed be thy name. Thy kingdom come.	Our Father which art in heaven, Hallowed be thy name. Thy king-

Sinai MS. (Aleph)	*A. V.*
Thy will be done, as in heaven, so also (also *marked by corrector for deletion*) on (*corrector adds* the) earth. (*Corrector inserts in margin,* And deliver us from the evil one.) Our daily bread give us day by day. And forgive us our sins as also (*corrected to* for also) we ourselves forgive every man that is indebted to us. And lead us not into temptation.	dom come. Thy will be done, as in heaven, so in earth. Give us day by day our daily bread. And forgive us our sins; for we also forgive every one that is indebted to us. And lead us not into temptation; but deliver us from evil.

[B has the following differences: 'Thy will be done, as in heaven, so also on earth' is omitted; B reads 'for we also ourselves forgive'; 'but deliver us from the evil one' is omitted. It will have been noticed that this clause was inserted by the corrector of Aleph at the wrong place. He originally began to write it, in the right margin, in the correct position, but changed his mind, washed out what he had written, and rewrote the words as above, altering 'but' to 'and'.]

Luke xxiii. 34. The words 'And (A.V. 'then') Jesus said, Father, forgive them, for they know not what they do', omitted by B, occur in Aleph, as in the Authorized Version.

John iv. 9–10. How is it that thou, being a Jew, askest drink of me, which am a woman of Samaria? Jesus answered and said, &c. The words, 'for the Jews have no dealings with the Samaritans', are inserted in Aleph by a corrector, but in B they are part of the original text.	How is it that thou, being a Jew, askest drink of me, which am a woman of Samaria? for the Jews have no dealings with the Samaritans. Jesus answered and said, &c.

John vii. 53–viii. 11 (consisting mainly of the episode of the woman taken in adultery) is omitted, as also by B and most of the earliest authorities.

Lastly, the reading of Aleph in Luke xxii. 43, 44 deserves special mention. The text of the Authorized Version has: 'And there appeared an angel unto him from heaven, strengthening him. And being in an agony he prayed more earnestly: and his sweat was as

20

it were great drops of blood falling down to the ground.' Both B and A omit these two verses entirely, but they occur, in the form just quoted, in Aleph. A corrector has, however, inserted the dots which were used as a sign of deletion; he had presumably found the verses wanting in another manuscript with which he compared this and decided that they were spurious. So much is evident from the facsimile, where some at least of the dots are quite clear; but a close scrutiny of the manuscript reveals what the facsimile does not, that either the same or some other corrector has attempted to erase the dots. In the spaces between the lines, where the use of the knife might endanger the actual text, he has been only partially successful, and several of the dots are visible, one or two being even untouched; but a magnifying glass shows that dots were also inserted in the left margin and that these have in fact been effectively erased, the vellum showing, however, the roughness of surface due to the knife.

This example provides an answer to a question asked by some critics: Why, since a complete facsimile of the Sinai manuscript exists, need the original be acquired? For the finer and more exact details of scholarship not even the best facsimile can ever replace an original manuscript. All who have done work of this kind know how often it happens that such problems as the identification of hands, the proper assignment of corrections, sometimes the very question whether a particular reading is original or a later correction, can be solved only by a minute examination of the actual manuscript; and in matters of textual criticism, notably in the case of Aleph, the authority to be attached to corrections, which depends largely on identification of hands, is often of high importance. To take but one point in illustration, Professor Kirsopp Lake, referring to this very manuscript, has said: 'In a MS. the sense of touch often helps to detect erasures, or the erosions of faded ink, and this is of course impossible in a photographic facsimile.'

It is thus a matter for rejoicing that the Trustees of the British Museum have been able to acquire this, one of the primary authorities for the text of the Bible. They already possessed the Codex Alexandrinus, besides some important manuscripts of the Syriac and Coptic versions, while the Codex Bezae, another of the primary authorities, is at Cambridge, and the Codex Ephraemi rescriptus and Codex Claromontanus are no farther away than Paris. Such concentration of early codices in a limited area is of the utmost service to scholars, who will thus be saved both time and expense in their researches.

The purchase from the Soviet Government was effected at the end of 1933, with the help of an advance by the Treasury, for £100,000, the British Government having undertaken to contribute £1 for every £1 contributed from other sources.

On Jan. 15 the Trustees of the British Museum appealed to the public for £50,000 to cover their liability in the matter, and so meet the Government's offer. This sum has now been secured; but a widespread wish has been expressed that the whole £100,000 should be raised by voluntary contributions, and a fresh appeal has been issued by the leaders of the Christian Churches in this country to all who reverence the Bible and realize its unique value in the moral and spiritual life of the nation, to do all they can to achieve this. The Trustees are cordially supporting this further appeal.

It may be added that the Russian Government is expending the amount of the price in the purchase of goods from Great Britain; and hence subscribers can feel that in sending their contributions they are helping not merely to acquire a valuable manuscript for the national library but to provide employment for British workmen.

In conclusion, thanks must be returned to the Oxford University Press, which has generously borne the cost of composition for this pamphlet, and to Messrs. Vaus and Crampton, who with equal generosity presented the blocks from which the illustrations were printed.

Subscriptions may be sent to the Director, British Museum, London, W.C. 1, or be handed in at any bank for transmission to the Westminster Bank, Bloomsbury Branch, London, W.C. 1, 'for the Sinai Bible Manuscript Account'.